Visual Design
for Online Learning

Jossey-Bass Guides to Online Teaching and Learning

Visual Design for Online Learning

Torria Davis

JB JOSSEY-BASS™

A Wiley Brand

Published by Jossey-Bass
A Wiley Brand
One Montgomery Street, Suite 1000, San Francisco, CA 94104-4594—www.josseybass.com

Jossey-Bass books and products are available through most bookstores. To contact Jossey-Bass directly call our Customer Care Department within the U.S. at 800-956-7739, outside the U.S. at 317-572-3986, or fax 317-572-4002.

Wiley publishes in a variety of print and electronic formats and by print-on-demand. Some material included with standard print versions of this book may not be included in e-books or in print-on-demand. If this book refers to media such as a CD or DVD that is not included in the version you purchased, you may download this material at http://booksupport.wiley.com. For more information about Wiley products, visit www.wiley.com.

Library of Congress Cataloging-in-Publication Data

Davis, Torria, 1966-
  Visual design for online learning/Torria Davis.—1
    pages cm
  Includes index.
  ISBN 978-1-118-92243-9 (paperback), 978-1-118-92245-3 (ePDF), 978-1-118-92244-6 (ePub)
  1. Internet in education. 2. Instructional systems--Design. 3. Visual communication. I. Title.
  LB1044.87.D384 2015
  371.33'44678—dc23

                              2015027458

Cover design by Wiley

Cover image: ©iStock.com/artishokcs

Printed in the United States of America
FIRST EDITION
PB Printing   10 9 8 7 6 5 4 3 2 1

CONTENTS

To my colleagues, near and far,
and to those I haven't met yet

PREFACE

In the year leading up to the writing of this book, I was blessed with the opportunity to view over two hundred courses for award nominations. The insights shared throughout the book have been gleaned from this experience and an ever-expanding professional network of educators, information technology professionals, web designers, and thought leaders from a multitude of disciplines, colleges, universities, and trade schools. Many of the courses created by these practitioners have earned the distinction of "exemplary course" from their colleagues in the teaching and learning community. What is an exemplary course? The term is commonly used among those in the Blackboard user group community. It refers to a voluntary peer-reviewed assessment process in which educators immersed in teaching and learning online provide their critique of courses built using any of the Blackboard learning management system of products. Blackboard's Exemplary Course Program began in 2000 to encourage the dissemination of best practices in course design, using a rubric developed by the program's directors and others from the Blackboard user community.

An exemplary course is in no way a perfect course. In fact, you will see many outstanding illustrations that do not comply with all aspects of the visual design ideas suggested in this book. The visual design of any course, mine included, is influenced by institutional policies, practices, and constraints unique to the context in which the course was developed. Therefore, the screenshots graciously contributed by faculty and leaders of instructional design throughout the United States, Canada, and the United Kingdom are presented for the strengths they exhibit. And that is good news! Courses do not have to be perfect to be awesome and effective. In the fast-paced space of course design for online delivery, we are all learning new design strategies with new tools seemingly introduced every day to the online teaching and learning market. I hope that the ideas presented will be a springboard that will launch our creativity and enhance the effectiveness of the courses we design.

WHAT WILL YOU LEARN?

Like a quartet in perfect harmony, good visual design of instructional content for online delivery is a blend of multimedia that facilitates readability, meaning making, and recall. This book is specifically about the visual representation of relevant and engaging content in a learning management system or website. To accomplish the aims of good visual design of a course or training, this book discusses the basic technology skills needed and the principles that undergird good teaching online. While there are other fundamental visual design concepts within the disciplines of fine and graphic art, and many theoretical underpinnings for learning theories, this book is meant to serve as a starting point for the course designer, developer, or trainer creating the basic visual design of a course or training for delivery through a learning management system or website.

The book is organized by questions commonly asked by faculty in their roles as online course designers, developers, and trainers. This means the book can be read chronologically by those designing their first course and topically by more experienced practitioners.

- Chapter One suggests how to begin conceptualizing the visual design of your course once the content has been determined.

- Chapter Two addresses issues of copyright, fair use, and strategies for searching the Internet for royalty-free images and video you may want to include in your online course or training.

- Chapter Three discusses visual designs for facilitating discussions and projects among students, providing guided instruction to online learners, and managing the amount of content provided in the course.

- Chapter Four suggests practical ways to integrate multimedia to engage online learners while enhancing the visual appearance of the content pages of a learning management system or website.

- Chapter Five applies everything discussed in the previous chapters to illustrate how a course can be constructed online using a logical and progressive sequence and to model the building of a four-week professional development course in a learning management system.

- Chapter Six suggests visual designs for supporting learners in the online environment.

If you're like me when I began visually designing courses, you're probably experiencing conflicting emotions. On the one hand, you're probably overwhelmed by the prospect of building a course in a learning management system or website. On the other hand, you're excited about the opportunity to learn the visual design skills needed to display, in all its grandeur, the content you've gathered and created. My recommendation is to use this text like a workbook. While you can certainly read the book chronologically and gain information, maximum benefit will be gained by immediately beginning to build your course in a platform of your choice. By doing so, you can practically apply the strategies and frameworks as they are discussed.

The visual design illustrations were selected for the representation of one or more best practices in course design, interaction and collaboration, assessment, and learner support. These categories make up the criteria for Blackboard's Exemplary Course Program rubric, a link to which is provided at http://www.torriadavis.com/visual-designs-for-online-learning. Throughout the book, common design challenges are presented in the context of these criteria, and the solutions offered can be applied to your design efforts. I fervently hope that you will not only use what you learn but also share it through as many venues as possible. With the rapid changes in technology, the best thing we can do for one another is share what we learn.

Just as iron sharpens iron, friends sharpen the minds of each other.
—Proverbs 27:17 (Contemporary English Version)

ACKNOWLEDGMENTS

"No man is an island unto himself" (John Donne, 1623) is often cited to express the interconnectedness of all people with one another. It is this interconnectedness that makes this book possible. I am able to share the ideas presented here because of the innovative environment in which I work, the expertise of IT professionals who entertained my questions and tolerated my learning curve, and the resources provided for me to experiment daily and collaborate with professionals across time and space.

Chief among these is the president of California Baptist University, Dr. Ronald Ellis. Although I have not had the pleasure of working with him directly, I experience the positive effects of his leadership every work day as he provides the direction and resources for the Online and Professional Studies Division. The following individuals are my favorites:

Dr. David Poole, my favorite vice president of the Online and Professional Studies Division. I appreciate the opportunity I've had to share web tools and other teaching strategies as he teaches online while leading a division committed to "The Great Commission."

Dr. Tran Hong, my favorite associate vice president of technology. He's been God's hands in my professional life. In my quest to mentor and support faculty as the only instructional designer for the division, Dr. Hong has never denied me a needed or innovative resource.

Dr. Dirk Davis, my favorite academic dean. He's been an excellent mentor to me. The online teaching skills I've learned and shared with our faculty are in part a result of his mentorship and the vision he has for the online learning experience of students.

The soon-to-be Dr. Robert Shields, my favorite online learning systems administrator. He is the calm in the midst of my "the computer is not doing what it's supposed to" storm. Whenever I frantically scream "Robeeeerrrrt! Help!" he calmly and patiently teaches me how to help myself.

This is also true of Kyle Howlett, my favorite web design developer. I have learned and am still learning how to manipulate iframes, and cascading style sheets (CSS). He's patient and empowering, and he reminds me to "ask Google."

I wish there were space to introduce you to the entire phenomenal group of faculty who teach for the Online and Professional Studies Division. At the time of this writing, the division has entered its fifth year, with forty-eight full-time faculty members. Their willingness to creatively work through pedagogical challenges with me makes it a joy to collaborate with them and experiment with ideas on their behalf. Much of what is shared in this book is the result of that collaboration and experimentation.

My professional practice has also been influenced by the professional associations from which I've gleaned resources and techniques. Because I am challenged to remember the names of *all* the workshop presenters and colleagues with whom I've engaged in online discussions and peer feedback, it's important for me to share the professional development experiences I've had as a new instructional designer over the past four and a half years, validating the impact of social learning theory (Bandura, 1971) on my professional development:

- @One: Building Community with Social Media 2011
- Computer Using Educators (CUE) Conference, Palm Springs, California 2011
- International Society for Technology Educators (ISTE) Conference, San Diego 2012
- LERN: Building Online Learning Communities 2012
- LERN: Designing Online Instruction 2012
- Quality Matters Rubric Standards and Workbook 2011–2013 Edition
- Association of Training and Development (ATD) 2013
- Video Maker Basics of Video Production 2013
- Blackboard Exemplary Course Program Volunteer Reviewer 2011–2013
- Blackboard Exemplary Course Program Director 2014
- BbWorld 2014 presenter and attendee
- Online Learning Consortium (formerly The Sloan Consortium)— Participated in the following online workshops 2012–2013:
  - Mobile Learning Mastery Series
  - Blended Learning Mastery Series

- Learning Environments: Teaching and Learning with Online Science Labs
- Successful Online Outcomes: Improved Discussions
- Strategies for Successful Group Work

The idea for this book was influenced in part by the collaborative experiences between the Online and Professional Studies Division and the Community Programs division of Blackboard Learn under the directorship of Sheryn Anthes. With the support of the executive leadership of both organizations, access to the Blackboard environments of institutions across continents is shared throughout the book. Many thanks are extended to the following instructional designers, faculty, directors, and university administrators who gave permission to use images from their Blackboard environments, and to the support staff and teams with whom each contributor collaborated.

Dr. Larysa Nadolny, Assistant Professor

Dr. Nadolny is an assistant professor at Iowa State University. Recent awards include an Early Achievement in Teaching Award and a Blackboard Catalyst award.

website: www.drnadolny.com/

Jan G. Neal, Lead Instructional Designer

Jan Neal is Embry-Riddle Aeronautical University's (ERAU) lead instructional designer for doctoral studies. Jan has designed and built numerous courses. She is a recipient of seven Blackboard Exemplary Course awards.

Jason Rhode, Ph.D.

Dr. Rhode is the director of the Faculty Development and Instructional Design Center for Northern Illinois University. He oversees all faculty development at NIU.

website: www.jasonrhode.com or www.niu.edu/facdev

Jennifer Perkins, Instructional Designer

Jennifer Perkins is an instructional designer for the Instructional Development Center of Eastern Kentucky University (EKU) Online. She supports faculty members in design and development of courses offered using EKU's e-Campus learning model.

website: http://jenperkins.com/

Dr. Jenny Yeo, Associate Clinical Lecturer

Dr. Yeo is an associate clinical lecturer in the faculty of medical sciences at Newcastle University. She is a module leader and is responsible for development and delivery of her modules, which are wholly e-learning in nature.

Lynne Rawles, Faculty of Medical Sciences E-Learning Coordinator

Lynne Rawles works at Newcastle University. Her course design collaboration with Dr. Jenny Yeo resulted in a 2014 Blackboard Catalyst award for an exemplary course.

Katie R. Evans, Manager of eLearning Instructional Design and Quality Assurance / Humanities Instructor

Katie Evans is a 2013 ECP award winner. She currently manages the instructional design team at Lake-Sumter State College in Florida and teaches online humanities courses.

website: https://twitter.com/KateEvansWrites

Katie Laubengayer, Curriculum Specialist

Katie Laubengayer is a curriculum specialist at Idaho Digital Learning Academy. Katie works with subject matter experts to develop online courses, specializing in copyright issues.

Matthew Acevedo, Instructional Designer

Matt Acevedo is an instructional designer with Florida International University Online. He specializes in collaborating with faculty to create effective and engaging learning experiences in higher education.

Dr. Riste Simnjanovski, Assistant Academic Dean

Dr. Simnjanovski is the assistant academic dean and an assistant professor for the Online and Professional Studies Division of California Baptist University in Riverside, California. He oversees all course development for the division.

Shannon Conley Kurjian, Social Studies Teacher

Shannon Conley-Kurjian is a fifteen-year high school educator interested in making digital natives digital learners. She teaches social studies at Medina High School in Medina County, Ohio.

Wendi M. Kappers, Ph.D.

Dr. Kappers is a network engineer and instructional designer with fifteen years of classroom experience and serves as the director for the Rothwell Center for Teaching and Learning Excellence (CTLE) of Embry-Riddle Aeronautical University.

Sara Ombres, M.Ed.

Sara Ombres is an experienced instructional designer and educational technologist and serves as the assistant director for the Rothwell Center for Teaching and Learning Excellence (CTLE) of the Embry-Riddle Aeronautical University Worldwide Campus.

Martin Carroll, Pro Vice-Chancellor, Academic

Professor Carroll is pro vice-chancellor at Charles Darwin University in the Northern Territory of Australia. He is a leader in academic quality assurance and a multi-award-winning international speaker, consultant, and author.

Jason Warnick, Associate Professor of Psychology

Professor Warnick is a fellow of the International Stress and Behavior Society and has received national recognition for online education and academic advising. He is an associate professor of psychology at Arkansas Tech University.

Sandra Bennett, Instructional Designer

Sandra Bennett is a twenty-three-year educator with over twelve years as an instructor at Wilmington University in Delaware and a 2013 Blackboard Catalyst Award winner for exemplary course development.

Elaine Ahumada, D.P.A

Dr. Ahumada is the associate professor of public administration, chair of history and government, and director of the masters in public administration for the Online and Professional Studies Division of California Baptist University in Riverside, California. Her scholarly interests include public administration, androgogy, leadership, and culture and gender issues.

website: www.cbuonline.edu/ops/FacultyDetails?id=8

Matthew Emerson, Ph.D.

Dr. Emerson is an assistant professor of Christian ministries and chair of arts and sciences for the Online and Professional Studies Division of California Baptist University in Riverside, California. His scholarly interests include biblical studies, theology, and interpretation.

website: www.cbuonline.edu/ops/FacultyDetails?id=13

Dirk Davis, Ed.D.

Dr. Davis is the academic dean and an associate professor of education for the Online and Professional Studies Division of California Baptist University in Riverside, California. His scholarly interests include distance learning and classroom management and discipline.

website: www.cbuonline.edu/ops/FacultyDetails?id=3

Elizabeth Morris, Ph.D.

Dr. Morris is an associate dean and associate professor of education for the Online and Professional Studies Division of California Baptist University in Riverside, California. Her scholarly interests include mathematics and math anxiety.

website: www.cbuonline.edu/ops/FacultyDetails?id=4

Gretchen Bartels, Ph.D.

Dr. Bartels is an assistant professor of English for the Online and Professional Studies Division of California Baptist University in Riverside, California. Her scholarly interest include rare books and manuscripts, as well as teaching composition and literature.

    website: www.cbuonline.edu/ops/FacultyDetails?id=31

Yvonne Thai, Ph.D.

Dr. Thai is an assistant professor and lead faculty of sociology for the Online and Professional Studies Division of California Baptist University in Riverside, California. Her scholarly interests include identity and identity processes, morality, altruism, organizations and institutions, religion, gender, and emotions.

    website: www.cbuonline.edu/ops/FacultyDetails?id=27

Monica O'Rourke, Ph.D.

Dr. O'Rourke is an assistant professor of kinesiology for the Online and Professional Studies Division of California Baptist University in Riverside, California. Her scholarly interest include national and international travel providing chaplaincy services to professional action sports athletes.

    website: www.cbuonline.edu/ops/FacultyDetails?id=46

Scott Dunbar, M.B.A.

Professor Dunbar is an assistant professor of human resource management for the Online and Professional Studies Division of California Baptist University in Riverside, California. He teaches courses in Human Resource Management, Business and Organizational Management, Management with Biblical Foundation, Business Policy And Strategy, Information System Essentials, and Business IT Applications.

    website: www.cbuonline.edu/ops/FacultyDetails?id=67

ABOUT THE AUTHOR

D r. Torria Davis is an accomplished educator with expertise in the areas of curriculum and course design for today's multigenerational adult learning audience. A published writer, researcher, presenter, and award-winning course designer, Dr. Davis shares her more than twenty years of experience in elementary, secondary, and post-secondary education. Her understanding of course management systems, learning theories, and instructional design principles is foundational to her mentorship of university professors in their efforts to incorporate technology and create interactive and engaging online courses for adult learners. This work is of the utmost importance to her because she believes, as stated by Peter Drucker, "We now accept the fact that learning is a lifelong process of keeping abreast of change. And the most pressing task is to teach people how to learn." Her scholarship can be read in peer-reviewed journals such as the *Journal for Childhood Education*, published by the Association for Childhood Education International; *Teachers College Record*; and the *Journal for Educational Considerations*, published by the College of Education at Kansas State University, as well as a chapter entitled "The Good Teacher" in Kidd and Chen's edited textbook *Ubiquitous Learning: Strategies for Pedagogy, Course Design, and Technology* (Information Age, 2011). Her understanding of the intersection between learning theories and instructional technologies is expressed regularly on her site at TorriaDavis.com. She earned her Ph.D. in education at Claremont Graduate University and currently serves as an instructional designer for the Online and Professional Studies Division of California Baptist University in Riverside, California.

1

HOW DO I BEGIN?

I strive for two things in design: simplicity and clarity.
—Lindon Leader

Don't do what I did! When I was a new instructional designer, I had the opportunity to collaborate with our academic administrative team to develop faculty workshops for teaching online. Initially those workshops were offered face-to-face, and we covered major topics like community building, course design, teaching techniques, and assessment. As our faculty grew and adjunct instructors were located farther away from our main campus, the academic administrative team began to consider blended and fully online workshop options. When I began to redesign the face-to-face course for fully online delivery, I wanted to make sure that faculty taking the workshops online, received the same benefit of our team's experiences as if we were all training together in a classroom. So I included in the redesign everything (and I do mean everything) we had shared in the face-to-face training. As a result, the first version of the online course looked like Figure 1.1. Folders contained folders that contained several content items and additional folders. Faculty practically needed to memorize the organizational scheme to find any one content item of interest. As the course developer, even I could not recall the organizational scheme I had created when I needed to direct faculty to a specific content item. Simplicity and clarity are important aims for designers in any field—and Figure 1.1 falls short of both aims.

To use a colloquial expression common among United States southerners, the course excerpt in Figure 1.1 is a "hot mess"! A hot mess describes anything in a state of extreme disorder or disarray. I don't mind poking fun at my earlier course design attempts. We all start somewhere,

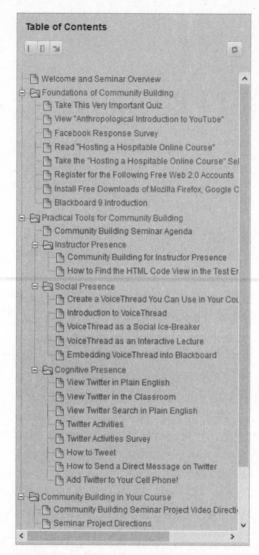

Figure 1.1 Too many technologies with excessive amounts of content take the focus away from course learning outcomes

and I was very proud of that hot mess after I built it. At that time, I was simultaneously learning the features of Blackboard, my institution's learning management system, and providing support to faculty as they taught and built courses online. So why would I say the example in Figure 1.1 is a hot M.E.S.S.? Four reasons:

- Many new technologies were rapidly thrust upon faculty in a short time span. This inadvertently drew the focus away from the learning objectives. Frustration set in as faculty attempted to use the technologies for the first time, navigate many content folders to locate needed resources, and apply the content.

- Excessive amounts of nice-to-know content flooded the course. Nice-to-know content is content that is not directly related to learning objectives. There is a vast amount of information available on any given topic. As course designers and developers, it's our responsibility to vet the information and use our professional judgment to select the one, two, or three resources that will best help a learner attain the desired outcomes of the course.

- Several related content items were created as individual resources. Creating individual content items for related resources can overwhelm learners with volumes of content and waste valuable study time with unnecessary clicks and page loading time.

- Supplemental resources mixed with required resources makes it difficult to differentiate important content from optional content. Label supplemental resources as optional so that learners can prioritize the resources needed to attain learning outcomes.

When all four of these issues are present in a content folder, learning module, or course, we take the focus away from course learning outcomes. Combined, these issues thwart development of any sense of learner self-efficacy by raising anxiety that hinders meaning making and creating clutter that steals time away from the learning task. This threaten retention and course completion by overwhelming students, particularly those who may be adjusting to learning online.

While I achieved my goal of packing into the course everything I thought we shared in the face-to-face training, I also guaranteed that faculty wouldn't be able to find any one thing for which they might be looking. Faculty trying to find a piece of content probably got the same knot in their stomach that I get when I'm looking for a specific item in the garage that has been packed away for a couple of years. Although the boxes in the garage are clearly labeled, I can never remember where one specific item is located. That is exactly what happened in the first few online workshops I designed for faculty. When faculty asked which folder a specific item was in, sometimes I couldn't remember. This can happen when there is a high "folder depth ratio." A high folder depth ratio occurs when content folders are nested in several layers of additional content folders. So the first thing I learned about course design was to keep the design light. To do this, I had to accept that online teaching is different from teaching face-to-face in a classroom—not better or worse, just different. While both delivery formats can offer high-quality content, interactions, and collaboration, they differ in how it's done. Both delivery formats can be rigorous and challenging but differ in the techniques and tools used to achieve the same end. Therefore, there is no need to fill the online space with an abundance of content and information. Instead, the goal is to design the online climate so that the opportunity for quality instruction, peer interactions and collaboration, rigor, and challenge is the same as in face-to-face classroom instruction.

So the question now becomes, how do you design an online environment where there are opportunities for quality instruction, peer interactions, collaboration, rigor, and challenge without opening the floodgates of massive amounts of content nested three and four folders deep? My suggestion: keep the course design light. Imagine the feeling you have when a burden has been lifted, a challenge has been surmounted, or a conflict is resolved—that light feeling you get when tension has been released through exercise, prayer, a massage, or a relaxing evening doing what you love to do. Learning something new or pursuing a goal come with tensions as you wrestle with new concepts. However, tensions shouldn't come from an abundance of material that hasn't been vetted properly. Tensions shouldn't come from not being able to find the resources you need to achieve what is expected. Tensions shouldn't come from the technology itself.

Keeping the course design light will help avoid the hot mess in Figure 1.1. What does it mean to keep a course light? First, the content presented is focused on specific objectives based on what you want the learner to do or consider at the conclusion of the course. The course navigation keeps the learner within a few clicks of any resource needed. Second, the learning technologies used are explained, supported, and kept to a minimum. The more technologies students are expected to use, the more content is required to explain and support the technologies used. Keeping the course design light facilitates a focus on learning outcomes, as follows:

1. Reducing the number of new technologies integrated into the course increases familiarity with required technologies, leaving students more mental energy for synthesizing course content.

2. Purging excessive amounts of content, whether assignments or resources, helps students manage their time on task.

3. Merging related content items contributes to a lower folder depth ratio, so students can more easily find what they need when they need it.

4. Separating required resources from optional resources focuses the learners' attention on the resources directly related to attaining learning objectives.

With that in mind, I'd like to highlight four basic technology skills that will facilitate a light course design. Using the acronym L.I.T.E. will help us to remember them. These foundational skills will be developed in the remaining chapters:

- Links—Create clickable links to external content.
- Integrate multimedia—Merge similar or related text, video, audio, still images, graphics, animation, hypermedia, simulations, and other types of interactive objects.
- Typography—Enhance readability and legibility by using fonts, font size, bullets, numbering, and line spacing to create white space.
- Embed—Display content at the point of need.

Keeping the design L.I.T.E. prevents a M.E.S.S. and also complements the Universal Design for Learning (UDL) framework, when applied to courses designed in a learning management system or website. The UDL framework advocates making content accessible to all learners, with and without disabilities (Center for Applied Special Technology, 2011). As disabilities can be both seen and unseen, the L.I.T.E. skills and the UDL framework provide a foundation from which to provide visual support to all learners as they access instructional materials online. Who do we mean by "all learners"? The UDL framework considers the needs of novices entering a new field of study; experienced practitioners formalizing their education; second-language learners acquiring the academic language of their discipline; young adults through mature seniors on the continuum of social, cultural, linguistic, and economic diversity: as well as students with varied learning styles. Because learners using various devices can customize online content, UDL encourages the representation of content in multiple formats that include auditory, visual, and text materials.

"Content is king!" You've probably heard this expression. Knowing what you want learners to be able to do at the end of a course or training is foundational. Developing learning outcomes and assessment and instructional materials that are aligned with one another precedes any and all design efforts. This book assumes you have a good understanding of course development. That being understood, text is not enough! As technology advances, you no longer have to become a webpage designer—or hire one—to create and share content on the Web. Free learning management systems and websites make it possible for professionals from all disciplines to build and share content they create. To have the content shared in the best possible light, everyone needs to know there is more to content design in a learning management system or website than putting words on a page.

So how do we begin to design a course or training for online delivery? Follow along with me on a short visualization exercise. Let's say you are in the market to purchase a home or lease an apartment. What do you want the neighborhood to look like? As you drive toward a particular home on the market, is the address clearly visible from the curb? When you approach the home, is the pathway to the door obvious? When you walk into the entryway of the home, how does it make you feel? As you tour each room of the house or apartment, can you see exactly where your home furnishings will go? That's how you begin with your design! Your learners have arrived at the course homepage. What do you want them to see? How do you want them to feel? Where do they go to access various areas of the course? Once you've answered questions like these, you're ready to consider the visual design of pages throughout your course.

The primary purpose of good visual design is not to make the content page of your learning management system or website pretty, although there is no doubt that an aesthetically pleasing course can have the same appeal as the plate arrangement and garnishes of a well-prepared meal. The purposes of good visual design for online courses and trainings are threefold:

- To create a sense of presence in the course (Akyol, Garrison, & Ozden, 2009)

- To make content accessible to diverse learners (Center for Applied Special Technology, 2011)

- To provide resources at the point of need

Learners want to know that (1) their instructor is a real person who cares about their success in the course and (2) there are other learners in the course with whom they can share perspectives. We'll discuss these facets of learning communities in the next chapter. Good design ensures that students know who the instructor is and how to contact the instructor. Students know the instructor is there for them when responses to inquiries are timely, feedback informs them of their progress toward learning outcomes, misconceptions are addressed, and dynamic instruction both models and encourages critical thinking among the learners. In addition, good design ensures that content items are accessible to students using a variety of computer and mobile devices, students with varied learning styles, students with a broad range of physical and mental abilities, and students covering the full spectrum of discipline-specific expertise. Lastly, good design removes distractions from the online environment. This is best done by providing the resources students need at the point of need. An online environment free from distractions means students are as close as possible to being one click away from a needed resource. If the visual design of a course fulfills these purposes, learners will experience the support they need to achieve the intended learning outcomes in a distance learning environment.

START WITH WHAT YOU KNOW

Before you panic and say you don't know anything and that's why you're reading this book, think about the computer skills you use every day. Do you use a word processor to outline a lesson plan or prepare a handout for students? What about a presentation program to provide visuals that supplement a lecture? Starting with what you know is a good way to build your confidence and experience small wins when it comes to visually designing a course in a learning management system or website. When I started as a new instructional designer, I came from the faculty ranks as an associate professor of teacher education, specifically in the secondary credential program. All I knew at that time were the basic functions of the Microsoft Office Suite. In planning instruction, I worked primarily with Word and PowerPoint. Those are great tools to build from. Here's what I mean.

Let's say I'm building an introduction to teaching course and I want to gather visuals for the perennialist philosophical perspective of teaching. Microsoft Word and PowerPoint are great applications with which to start. Figure 1.2 shows where to find images in Word. After selecting a picture, I can use the Windows 7 Snipping Tool to screenshot the clip art and save it as an image. To locate the Snipping Tool, navigate to the Start menu, locate Programs and Accessories, or click inside the search field and type "Snipping Tool." Later the background can be removed in PowerPoint (Figure 1.3) and the image can be used to design a graphic that can be uploaded as a content item. Did you already know that? Awesome! Let's apply what you know to building a content item in a learning management system (LMS). Compared to building a content item with text alone, Figure 1.4 shows three ways to use the graphic in an LMS. The first image in Figure 1.4 is simply unformatted text. However, we've already agreed that text is not enough. The second image in Figure 1.4 is a picture by itself. While the picture gives clues to the definition of perennialism as a teaching philosophy, there is more that we can do. Let's move the image into PowerPoint. Since I am not a graphic artist, I can take advantage of the many layouts and themes to create an original image. After selecting a layout, the picture is imported and the background is removed, using

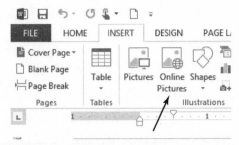

Figure 1.2 The Online Pictures icon in Microsoft Office applications allows for the convenient integration of images in instructional materials

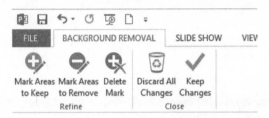

Figure 1.3 Until you develop Photoshop skills, use PowerPoint to remove image backgrounds for a transparent background

PowerPoint's background removal features, as shown in Figure 1.3. The objectives are added to the slide to focus the learner on the expected outcomes, as shown in the third image in Figure 1.4. The last image in Figure 1.4 is the title page layout. Not a bad design for a newbie, is it? This is a great beginning if you find yourself in the position of building courses with no background in design.

I took the following steps to create the images in Figure 1.4:

1. In PowerPoint 2013, access the online pictures from the "Insert" tab, and search for a desired image. If you have an earlier version of PowerPoint, the steps may differ.

2. Once the image is in PowerPoint, select the image and access the "Background Removal" feature located on the "Format" tab as shown in Figure 1.3.

3. Using the "Mark Areas to Keep" and "Mark Areas to Remove" buttons, click-and-drag, or trace the portion of the image you want to manipulate.

Perennialism

In this unit you will:
Define perennialism.
Identify advantages and disadvantages of perennialism.
Create a floor plan for a perennialist classroom.

Perennialism

Perennialism

In this unit you will:
· Define perennialism
· Identify advantages and disadvantages of perennialism
· Create a floor for the perennialist

Perennialism

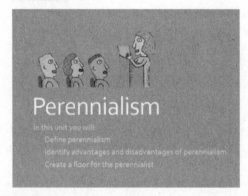

Figure 1.4   Four ways to create a visual for an instructional unit presented online

4. Once you have modified the image to your satisfaction, deselect the image and move it into the desired position on the slide.

5. Add formatted text as desired.

6. Save the slide, using the "Save as" feature on the "File" tab.

7. Use "Save as type" to change from PowerPoint Presentation to PNG.

Now that the PowerPoint slide is a PNG image, you are ready to import the image into the LMS or onto your website.

DESIGNING CONTENT PAGES

To create the look and feel you desire for your course, you will be designing different types of content pages. A content page contains the information that learners need to pursue learning outcomes. Four types of pages are common: the "landing page," "navigation page," "instructional page," and "assignment submission page." These pages are the bases from which students will perceive the instructor's presence in the online environment and receive the resources needed to achieve learning outcomes. As such, each type of content page serves a specific function.

The Landing Page

Just as your impression of a home or apartment is influenced by its curb appeal, the landing page sets the tone of the course. It's the first page students see, where they form their first impressions. When students arrive on the landing page, it's the instructor's first opportunity to make them feel welcome and provide the information needed to begin the course. Students will have many questions when they enter the course. How do I contact my instructor? Where is the course syllabus? What are the required texts for the course? What assignments are due, and when? The landing page is where many of these questions are addressed, with the first manifestation of the instructor's presence. Consider adding a picture of yourself (smiling!), accompanied by a welcome note written in the first person, which conveys warmth and hospitality. Some learners may enter the course with anxiety about the content or the online environment, and the smiling face of the instructor, with a welcome note, presents the instructor as personable and approachable.

The following are the steps taken to create the soft-edge effect on a portrait, as seen in Figure 1.5, that you might use to display a picture of yourself.

1. In PowerPoint, click the Picture icon on the "Insert" tab and navigate to a portrait of yourself.

2. Once the portrait is in PowerPoint, select the portrait and click the "Format" tab.

3. On the "Format" tab, you'll see the "Picture Styles" group. Locate and select the oval with soft edges.

4. To save the picture for later use, right-click the portrait and select "Save as Picture."

Now you're ready to upload the picture in the LMS or onto a website. Using tables to format images and text, as seen in Figure 1.5, is discussed in Chapter 5.

A well-designed landing page will introduce the instructor and answer the basic how-to-get-started questions that students need to know to begin the course. The landing page in Figure 1.5 displays a picture of the professor and suggests how to begin the course: by viewing a course introduction video, a syllabus review video and participating in the introductory discussion board activity. All of these items are accessible from the Week Zero folder, clearly visible under the instructor's welcome as part of the landing page. Some professors include a screencasted orientation or welcome video on the landing page such as the one in Figure 1.6.

Upon reviewing many online courses, it's clear that the landing pages of exemplary courses tend to share several attributes. Among the first content items encountered are an instructor picture, welcome message, or video message. And among these items, an overview of the course could be provided along with a screencasted video of the LMS user interface. In addition to a screenshot of a professor's embedded video message, Figure 1.6 shows a banner related to the course content. Banner, whether provided with publisher text materials or created with graphic design web tools,

Figure 1.5   The landing page is the first page students see in an online course

serve as a visual confirmation that the learner has accessed the correct course in the LMS. This serves the same purpose as writing the course and instructor name on the whiteboard on the first day of a face-to-face class. The landing page also provides guidance on how to proceed after arriving. The learner's eye instinctively scans the landing page looking for where

Figure 1.6 Landing page with professor welcome video embedded
Image courtesy of Martin Carroll from Charles Darwin University

to go next. Therefore, it's a good idea to make sure access to instructional materials is readily apparent on the landing page; say, by way of a link on a side menu or embedded in the text of the content page.

The Navigation Page

Another type of page that differs in function from the landing page is the navigation page. This provides access points to instructional materials and resources in the online environment. They can be links on a sidebar, as seen in Figure 1.7, or links in the table of contents, as seen in Figure 1.8. Navigation pages can lead to a single page of content or a single page with additional points of access to content. For example, the course menu in Figure 1.5 contains a link to learning activities. The learning activities link leads to a page that accesses several learning modules. In contrast, the syllabus link leads to one specific content page. For regularly accessed content, links on a sidebar or table of contents provide quick and convenient access points—a very common attribute among exemplary courses.

Navigation pages can also function as a landing page, as seen in Figure 1.5. Providing a single page as both a landing page and navigation page reduces the number of clicks needed to access a single piece of content,

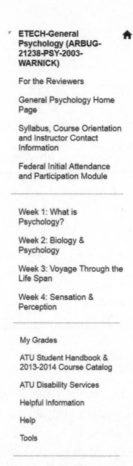

Figure 1.7 A course menu with a grouped navigation scheme allowing quick access to the links from anywhere in the course

Image courtesy of Jason Warnick from Arkansas Tech University

which minimizes page loading time and increases the learner's time on task. Navigation pages in exemplary courses tend to have short, descriptive link titles as seen in Figure 1.5; some use a grouped navigation scheme as seen in Figure 1.7. A grouped navigation scheme for the sidebar course menu is helpful when accessing related items. Notice that the course menu is divided into three parts—course information links, instructional units, and additional student resources. Because of the related groupings, learning modules are easy to access from any place within the course, as are the course syllabus and student grades.

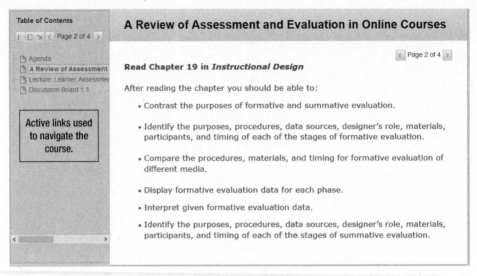

Figure 1.8 Reading objectives displayed on an instructional content page

The Instructional Page

An instructional page calls for different considerations from the landing and navigation pages. Instructional pages contain content to facilitate the attainment of learner outcomes. This might include course objectives, lectures, reading assignments, supplemental resources, and assessment activities. Any task a learner is asked to read, watch, review, and complete will be designed as an instructional page. Organization and planning of instructional pages differs considerably from the organization and planning of a face-to-face course. In a face-to-face course, you can begin with an outline or tentative agenda for weekly sessions and fine-tune those plans as the course unfolds, based on the interactions with students. With online class preparation, absolutely every detail—all directions, student resources, plans for interactions—is laid out before the class begins. If you begin with the end in mind, you can identify the sequential steps or objectives that must be attained in order to achieve the final learning outcome. Once you have segmented the final learning outcome into learning objectives, you can develop small instructional units, align learning objectives with instructional resources and assessments, and design individual instructional pages.

There are several best practices for designing instructional pages that have been gleaned from the voluntary peer review process of exemplary courses. Instructional pages generally include identification of measurable and observable goals and objectives; presentation of instructional content in well-sequenced, manageable lessons, units, or modules; and fostering of higher-order thinking for learner engagement. Course goals and objectives are usually located in the course syllabus. However, they can also be built into the LMS or website. Figure 1.5 shows the learning objectives displayed on the outside of the week one learning module. Figure 1.8 shows the reading objectives on the first page in a unit folder. Best practices in the online space suggest that goals and objectives should be explicitly stated in multiple areas in the course.

Instructional pages are also the pages that provide learners with just-in-time support at the point of need. If a learner needs to view a video, ideally the video will be embedded on the page with a Play button so the learner can view the video without navigating to any other location, as shown in Figure 1.9. If a learner needs to participate in a discussion forum, the access point to that discussion is provided on the page where the discussion is introduced. Whenever possible, avoid asking learners to click to other areas of the course to access a required resource. This risks frustrating learners if they can't locate the resource.

The Submission Page

The submission page serves as a repository for student work. As such, the page may contain a text editor for typing directly on the submission page or a link to upload files from the student's computer. Depending on the features available in the LMS or website, you may have submission pages for assignments, discussion forum responses, journal entries, blog posts, and wiki pages. Submission pages may communicate with the LMS's grade center function or contain submit buttons linked to the instructor's e-mail address. Figure 1.9 shows a submission page where a student will upload a completed project. To enhance navigation and minimize excessive content links, the submission area provides access to the project lecture in the same place where the finished project will be uploaded.

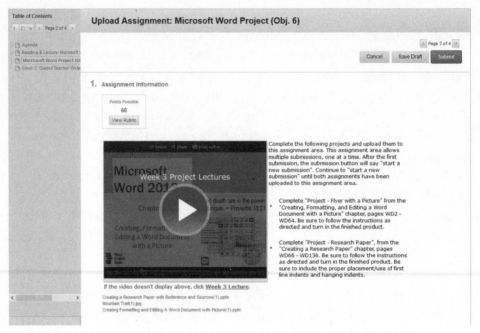

Figure 1.9   Instructional page with related instructional materials in one content item; the page also functions as a submission page

In addition, a PowerPoint file with slide notes is used as a lecture transcript in the same location to enhance accessibility to the curriculum. The PowerPoint file is free of transitions and animation so those using assistive devices can access the content. Furthermore, in case the lecture is not visible, a labeled link to the lecture is provided in a format accessible to screen readers.

KEEP THE DESIGN L.I.T.E.

Although each content page serves different specific functions, simplicity and clarity are the important aims for all content pages. Let's look at the ways in which the L.I.T.E. skills help us avoid a M.E.S.S. in the design of an online course or training. The technology skills of creating active links, integrating related multimedia content, using typography to create white space, and embedding resources at the point of need are the basic skills required to keep the course design L.I.T.E. By using these technology skills we can manage the folder depth ratio, eliminate excessive content, streamline related content, and support learner access, thereby avoiding a M.E.S.S.

Link to Content

Let's say I wanted to e-mail you the recipe for my favorite holiday dessert. When I type the e-mail, I have two options. First, I could list the ingredients and describe step-by-step how to make the recipe from scratch. This option would make the e-mail very lengthy. The recipe might seem complicated and discourage you from attempting it. The second option would be to e-mail you a list of ingredients, followed by directions of three to four short sentences explaining how to combine and bake the ingredients. To ensure that you understood all the nuances of preparing the recipe correctly, I could create links in the e-mail to vital information. For example, the ingredients list might show "4 eggs, separated" as a link. When you click on the link in the body of the e-mail, it might take you to a short video demonstration of separating egg yolks from whites. I might link the phrase "double boiler" in the recipe steps to a picture of a double boiler on the Web, with directions for use. Linking to external content allows me to explain the recipe instructions simply and clearly while providing the additional information you need but may not know.

Here's another example. Figure 1.10 shows an assignment exercise. While I have the option of using direct instruction, to embed a lecture that explains how to choose a computer, buy a webcam, or understand computer specifications, Figure 1.10 shows a preference for a constructivist's discovery approach to engaging the learner with course content. This approach encourages learners to construct meaning from the interactions they have with instructional materials and conversations with peers and experts (Bain, 2004). The image of the PowerPoint slide contains a text description of the objective for the exercise. The image is hyperlinked to an instructor-narrated video of the guided exercise. Below the image are

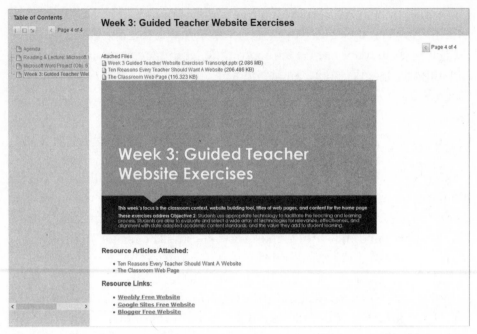

Figure 1.10 Linking to external content and attaching instructional files to the same content item encourages a constructivist approach to achieving a learning objective

several clickable resource links that learners use to explore the learning objective. The page requires minimal scrolling, as it contains everything the learner needs, including a transcript of the instructor-created video.

Integrate Multimedia and Similar Content Items

I remember back in the day when I could travel without being charged for one or two pieces of luggage. Aside from packing everything I needed for a trip, I packed everything I thought I *might* need. Like extra sweaters and a parka in case it got cold at Lake Havasu in July. Now that airlines are charging to check luggage, I've learned to pack only what I need into a carry-on for trips of less than five days. I can get five days of clothes and vanity items into a backpack. Roll those shirts, jeans, and undergarments tightly, so they take up as little space as possible, and I can still fit in my small tablet for in-flight entertainment. Similarly, integrating multimedia and merging related instructional items allows you to manage the appearance and number of items in a learning module.

The visual benefits of linking to external content are exponential when multiple content items are integrated into one. Compare Figure 1.1 (my M.E.S.S.) with Figure 1.11. Figure 1.1 shows a folder labeled "cognitive presence," with eight separate content items related to Twitter. There's a content item to explain what Twitter is, what a Twitter Search is, and how these might be used in the classroom. There is also a Twitter survey and a list of Twitter activities with directions on how to tweet, how to send a direct message, and how to add Twitter to your cell phone. If you're a faculty member who doesn't tweet, eight content items on an unfamiliar web tool may be overwhelming and discouraging. In contrast, Figure 1.11 shows seven of the eight content items integrated into one. One content item now contains a video explanation of Twitter and Twitter Search; two linked documents contain hyperlinks to Twitter use in the classroom, Twitter activities, cell phone usage with Twitter, and directions to perform basic Twitter functions. Wow, how refreshing! If the faculty member doesn't tweet, it may be easier to remain open-minded about Twitter use in the classroom if there is only one content item on the topic. Notice in Figure 1.11 that the vertical scroll bar has been removed from the table of contents as a result of linking to content and integrating multimedia and similar content items.

Use Typography and White Space

We see the printed word almost everywhere we look. Big print. Small print. Bold print. Italicized print. Decorative print. Serif and sans-serif print. So much so that we take for granted the white space around the words or graphics (Williams, 2008). It's tempting to see white space as wasted space or space that begs to be filled with something, anything. This notion couldn't be further from the truth.

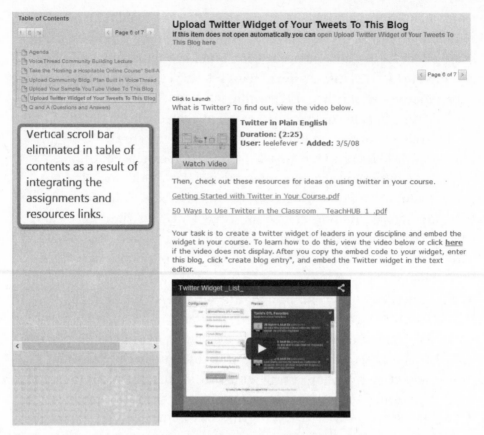

Figure 1.11 Linking to external content and integrating related content items minimizes feelings of being overwhelmed with unfamiliar content

There are some basic typographic elements common to course design in a learning management system or website. Typically, a "what you see is what you get" (WYSIWYG) editor allows you to manage point size, line spacing, line length, and font choice fairly easily. These same tools create white space (Vai & Sosulski, 2011). Why would we want to leave unused space on a content page? There are several reasons. For one, white space helps to draw attention to important content on a page. This could be section headers, key words or phrases, or graphics. White space also enhances readability, allowing you to scan a page for specific sections of

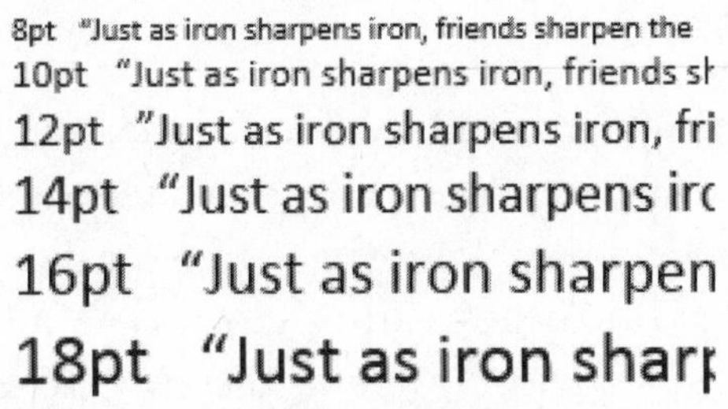

8pt "Just as iron sharpens iron, friends sharpen the

10pt "Just as iron sharpens iron, friends sh

12pt "Just as iron sharpens iron, fri

14pt "Just as iron sharpens iro

16pt "Just as iron sharpen

18pt "Just as iron shar

Figure 1.12 Line spacing and length, and font style and size contribute to readability through the creation of white space

text for example. When used well, we don't notice the typography or the white space, just the content on the page.

How can basic typography tools of point size, line spacing, line length, and font choice create white space? The smaller the font size, the less white space is created, and reading fluently becomes a challenge. Using a 12- to 14-point font is fairly standard, according to style formatting guidelines like APA (American Psychological Association) and MLA (Modern Language Association). Compare the point sizes in Figure 1.12. Single line spacing is also common when reading on a computer screen, as double spacing can force excessive scrolling. However, for longer bodies of text, 1.5 to double spacing is common between paragraphs. Again, this creates white space that enhances readability. Line length can be managed by breaking out numbered or bulleted lists rather than itemizing a list in running text. The indents associated with numbered or bulleted lists create white space that contributes to a balanced appearance and content organization.

Heading styles are a typical feature in WYSIWYG editors. Heading styles have associated line spacing. Most WYSIWYG editors come with only a few basic fonts like Verdana, Courier, Geneva, Helvetica, and Arial. Unless there is a specific reason to stray from these, stick with the classic fonts for legibility—that is, the readability of individual letters. The population as a whole is spending more time looking at computer screens (Greenfield, 2014). Decorative fonts are not easy to read for extended periods of time, so their use should be kept to a minimum for academic and training purposes.

Embed Content

Some time ago, my daughters and I went to the theatre to see a musical. As we approached the entrance, one of my daughters suggested we go to a mini market to purchase some candy and gum for the intermission. Although we arrived at the theatre early, there was no mini market or gas station with a mini market within walking distance. When we walked into the theatre, we noticed the concession stand in the center of the foyer. As we expected, the prices were outrageous: a small bag of peanut M&Ms cost $5. You'd think we'd walk away appalled at such an outrageous price. Instead, we laughed at ourselves for not being prepared, paid the $5, and enjoyed every one of those peanut M&Ms. Why? Convenience. Given our failure to come prepared, we saved ourselves time and energy by purchasing the conveniently available—albeit high-priced—candy.

Similarly, embedding content in your course makes content convenient to access and provides learner support in the online environment, helping learners use their study time efficiently. To effectively embed content means the material is visible and ready to view at the point of need. Technically all content, whether displayed as a link or text, is embedded. However, when we use the term "embed" in this context, we're referring to content that is visible at the point where the user encounters it. For example, Figures 1.9 and 1.11 show an embedded video. The user just needs to click the Play button to view the content in the location where it's presented, versus clicking on a link that opens in a new window or cutting and pasting an unclickable URL into a separate browser window. Embedding content reduces the number of clicks needed to access the content. Reducing the number of clicks saves page loading time, which will vary for students based on internet connection speeds and usage demands. Reducing time spent in noninstructional actions leads to better time management, which is particularly important to working adults with families. Figure 1.13 shows where embed codes should be placed. Look for an HTML icon, toggle switch, or widget in your content building environment.

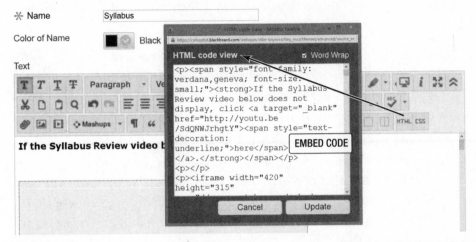

Figure 1.13 The text editor in a Blackboard Learn environment contains an HTML icon in which to copy and paste the embed codes from a variety of web tools

SUMMARY

In this chapter we discussed beginning the visual design of an online course or training by understanding the types of pages used in a course. The landing, navigation, instructional, and submission pages each serve a unique function in the course and should be designed with simplicity and clarity in mind. This can be achieved through the four basic technology skills needed to visually design a course in a learning management system or website. These skills were presented using the acronym L.I.T.E. for being able to *link*, *integrate*, use *typeface*, and *embed* content.

WHAT'S NEXT?

There are many learning management systems on the market, some proprietary, some free. In addition, many free websites are template driven. Both types of course design platforms come with text editors that vary in the features they offer. Identify a learning management system or website in which to build a course and make sure you can do the following in the platform you choose:

1. Create a link to external content. Words, phrases, or images can be used to create links to websites, e-mail addresses, and internal content. Most text editors contain a Link icon like the one shown here.

2. Locate embed codes. Typically this will be a link that indicates "sharing," followed by the word "embed." You'll often see a Share icon followed by multiple options. Although Share icons vary in appearance and embed codes vary in length, the following graphics illustrate what a Share icon and an Embed icon might look like.

Share icons   Embed icon

3. Locate the font, point size, and line spacing functions in your text editor. These basic tools help create white space and contribute to readability. The appearance of icons will vary, but you're looking for an icon with a single printed letter, a drop-down menu of point sizes, and a Line Spacing icon with three or four horizontal lines with vertical directional arrows. Not all text editors contain these features, and they may not be readily visible. However, it's important to know what tools you have to work with from the outset.

4. Locate features in the text editor that affect line length, such as numbered lists, bullets, and indents.

5. Practice asking Google. If you can't find it or figure it out, ask Google! When I first started working as an instructional designer, I would constantly ask my web developer colleague tech questions. His response was often "Did you Google it?" This was my first lesson in tech independence. Google is capable of returning decent search results even when you type a run-on sentence like "where on earth is a Blackboard tutorial on the text editor."

2

HOW DO I INCLUDE IMAGES AND VIDEO?

Only when the design fails does it draw attention to itself; when it succeeds, it's invisible.
—John D. Berry

I once celebrated my birthday with family members at a restaurant. At the end of our meal, the waitress brought a complimentary hot fudge sundae with all the toppings to the table. She lit a candle in the middle of the sundae and called all the available wait staff over to my table, where the group proceeded to sing the popular song "Happy Birthday to You" to the traditional tune from the late 1800s. It's a tradition to celebrate birthdays at restaurants, but over time I have noticed that at some restaurants staff are singing different happy birthday songs to fun tunes I hadn't heard before, and with different lyrics. If you're like me, you probably didn't know that "Happy Birthday to You" is a copyrighted song owned by an investment group. If restaurants perform the song for their patrons, the performance could be considered an infringement of copyright and the restaurant could be liable for royalty fees to the copyright holder. As it stands, the song's copyright expires in 2030.

Consider this. On Friday, February 7, 2014, in the Los Feliz area of Los Angeles, California, comedian Nathan Fielder opens a coffee shop under the name "Dumb Starbucks Coffee." The coffee shop uses the familiar Starbucks registered trademark, green color scheme, and product naming conventions, and even sells trendy "dumb" tumblers and jazz CDs just like the Seattle-based Starbucks Coffee. It's said that some customers waited up to three hours in line for a taste of the "dumb coffee" sold in the "dumb tall," "dumb grande," and "dumb venti" sizes (Schaefer, 2014).

The comedian's attorneys argue that adding the word "dumb" is making fun of the Starbucks coffee chain and, as a parody, is therefore considered "fair use" (Pritchard, 2014). Of course, everyone is asking the question: how is this legal?

This chapter is not intended to debate the issues surrounding perceived copyright infringements for performing the Happy Birthday song in a restaurant or the fair use argument of the Dumb Starbucks coffee shop. As a matter of fact, nothing written here about copyright and fair use laws constitutes legal advice. I am not an attorney and am not qualified to render a legal opinion about the application of copyright laws and fair use. It is the reader's sole responsibility to determine how copyright laws and fair use apply to any given context.

Whew! Now that *that's* out of the way . . .

As course designers, we don't want to open up a shop or sing a public performance of Happy Birthday in a restaurant. We simply want to add relevant images and video to our courses to facilitate the teaching and learning process in a discipline or training environment. Given the collaborative and sharing nature of information online, the question facing course designers and trainers is fairly straightforward: Can I use *this* material in my course or training? With the proliferation of online communities and web-based applications, the answer to this question can be ambiguous and subject to legal interpretation. If we understand that most of the time such lawsuits are filed because an individual or corporation feels slighted, cheated, or victimized in some way, a course designer might try to answer the question from the intended perspective of copyright rather than the legal perspective. Since the intended purpose of copyright law is to protect the rights of creators to benefit financially from their work, consider the following principles to live by:

- Treat others as you want to be treated.
- Consider the interest of others, not just your own.

Not rocket science, but profound nonetheless. If we respect the idea that authors and artists have a legal right to decide how their work is used, and if we quickly resolve perceived slights, we can minimize legal battles or avoid them altogether. From a viewpoint of empathizing with content creators, the question becomes, "Am I infringing upon the rights of another by using *this* content?" Let's explore what copyright is, the intentions of fair use laws as they pertain to copyrighted works, what constitutes copyright infringement, and the advent of Creative Commons licensing to facilitate the legal sharing of information found on the Web.

WHAT ARE COPYRIGHT AND FAIR USE?

According to the U.S. Copyright Office, "copyright" literally means "the right to copy." It represents the protections of law given to authors regarding the reproduction, distribution, public performance or showing, derivative works, and the licensing to others to use a work under specific terms and conditions (U.S. Copyright Office, n.d.). The purpose of these protections is to allow authors to benefit financially from intellectual creativity.

In contrast, the "doctrine of fair use" places limitations on the rights granted to authors through the copyright law for the purpose of allowing

- Criticism
- Comment
- News reporting
- Teaching
- Scholarship
- Research

On the surface, the law seems to suggest that copyrighted works can be "copied" or reproduced without permission or the payment of royalty fees for one of these purposes. But doing so could actually be considered an infringement of copyright subject to fines, imprisonment, or both.

In contrast to copyrighted work and fair use exceptions are works that are part of the "public domain." These works are not subject to copyright restrictions and are available to anyone without limits to use, share, and remix. For example, works created as a function of local, state, or federal government are part of the public domain (USA.gov, 2015). However, the privacy rights of the *subject* of the work may prevent its use. Works created after 1977 could enter the public domain as soon as seventy years after the creator's death. There are many stipulations regarding works in the public domain. To explore this topic further, you can visit the U.S. Copyright Office website or Google "public domain" for details.

WHAT IS COPYRIGHT INFRINGEMENT?

Simply put, copyright infringement occurs when a copyrighted work is copied or reproduced without legal permissions. An author's rights are in force from the moment a work is created, whether registered or not. Because copyrighted works do not have to be registered, it can be difficult to ascertain when copyright infringement has taken place. Section 107 of the copyright law suggests four factors that form the basis from which a decision of copyright infringement is argued:

1. The purpose and character of the use, including whether such use is of a commercial nature or is for nonprofit educational purposes;
2. The nature of the copyrighted work;
3. The amount and substantiality of the portion used in relation to the copyrighted work as a whole; and
4. The effect of the use upon the potential market for or value of the copyrighted work.

Given the six "fair use" exceptions to the rights given to authors through copyright laws, and the four factors listed in Section 107, it's clear that the ambiguity in the language of the law leaves room for legal interpretation. Before copying or reproducing copyrighted material, ask yourself whether you would want the same done to you and whether you are disregarding the interest of someone else. By understanding the intentions of the copyright law and empathizing with the copyright holder, you can minimize or avoid legal conflict.

THE TEACH ACT

For those teaching for accredited non-profit or governmental agencies, the Technology Education and Copyright Harmonization (TEACH) Act establishes guidelines to protect copyrighted works from inappropriate distribution within the educational and governmental industries (American Library Association, 2014). The TEACH Act, which became law in November 2002, establishes the conditions under which nonprofit educational and government agencies can use copyrighted works without permission or the payment of royalties (Crews, 2010). A complete discussion of the TEACH Act is beyond the scope of this chapter. The essence of the TEACH Act describes a context of use similar to the privileges granted in face-to-face class settings. To take advantage of the affordances of the TEACH Act, educational institutions and government agencies are asked to have published copyright policies that are actively disseminated in the academic or government community. They are also asked to restrict access to copyrighted work to the specific audience for which it is intended.

Still not clear on whether or not you can use a specific copyrighted work? Don't be too hard on yourself. The language in the law is the foundation for legal arguments on issues of copyright infringement and is not intended to provide a definitive answer for all contexts. What might a course designer or trainer do when irrefutable action is not clear? This is where the guided principles suggested earlier can help. Consider the following actions:

- Consult your institution's policies, and operate within those guidelines. Large educational and corporate institutions have access to legal counsel on these matters.

- Consider the documented policies and practices of institutions similar to yours. For example, when I google "copyright + fair use + university," several university institutions' documented policies appear in the search results. You can research how other institutions address the use of copyrighted works for teaching and learning.

- Consider what service organizations have to say about fair use. For example, a search for "code of best practices in fair use" will return search results from various organizations and documented brochures related to the use of different types of multimedia. You might also google "fair use + video" or another specific genre such as music or poetry.

- When in doubt, ask permission, consult an attorney, or don't use the material in question. One thing that is certain about copyright law is that authors have the right to determine how their work is used or displayed.

CREATIVE COMMONS

In 2001, the non-profit organization Creative Commons was founded to allow content creators to indicate how their work can be used or shared by others. On one extreme is copyright law, by which content creators reserve all rights to their work. On the other extreme is the public domain, by which content creators give up all rights to their work (or lose it with the passage of time). Creative Commons licenses are the middle ground, allowing content creators to retain *some* rights to their work. Through free copyright licenses, Creative Commons provides a standardized way for content creators to grant others permission to share, reuse, and remix their work provided they do so under the conditions stipulated by the content creator. Creative Commons offers six types of licenses based on the permissions that content creators want to extend to the public. These permissions can include sharing a work with attribution, sharing a work and making derivatives of that work, and sharing your work for commercial or noncommercial purposes. Figure 2.1 shows a typical Creative Commons license indicating permission to use content with attribution for noncommercial purposes. For a complete list and explanation of licenses available, google Creative Commons, and visit their website.

Figure 2.1 Representative icons depicting permissions granted through Creative Commons licenses

DETERMINING COPYRIGHT

Subject matter experts need to be able to download, save, and distribute images and instructional content digitally. How does an instructor determine whether or not a particular piece of content may be used in their course? Katie Laubengayer, a curriculum specialist at Idaho Digital Learning Academy, works with subject matter experts to develop online courses and specializes in copyright issues. According to Laubengayer, information about copyright can be found in several places. The quickest way to find copyright information is to look at the bottom of the web page displaying the content. If content is available under a Creative Commons license, you will often see the licensing information listed there, as shown in Figure 2.2. You might also find copyright information described in "Terms of Use," "Copyright," "Licensing Info," or "About Us" documents that may also be located at the bottom of a web page.

One source of images with readily accessible copyright information is the Wikimedia Commons site, a repository of media files contributed to the public domain under various Creative Commons licenses. Clicking on the images found on the Wikimedia sites will generally lead to a link detailing allowed uses. For example, a Google search on President Obama led to a Wikimedia Commons page with an image of President Obama behind a podium giving a speech. Copyright information was available

Figure 2.2 Image with Creative Commons license information located at the bottom of the web page displaying the content
Image courtesy of Katie Laubengayer from Idaho Digital Learning Academy

upon clicking the image, an excerpt of which is shown in Figure 2.3. With regards to works of the United States government, such as an image of President Obama found on the Wikimedia Commons site and linked from the White House blog, copyright protection is generally not available. A "'work of the United States Government' is a work prepared by an officer or employee of the United States Government as part of that person's official duties" (U.S. Copyright Office, n.d.). So, if you want to include images from a government website, the odds are in your favor that the content is in the public domain and will have copyright information accessible as in Figure 2.3.

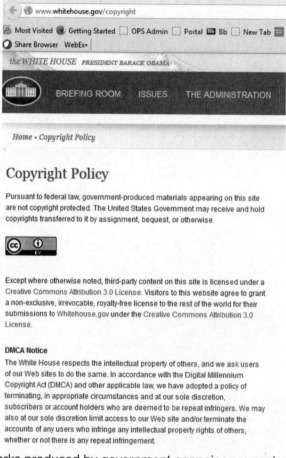

Figure 2.3 Works produced by government agencies are part of the public domain

WHERE CAN I FIND IMAGES?

Remember how, in Chapter One, you visualized yourself in the market for a new house or apartment? Now, let's say you've secured your home and it's time to decorate it. Where might you go to find decorative items? Maybe a favorite art gallery comes to mind. You're well aware that if you purchase an item there, you'll pay top dollar for a one-of-a-kind artwork to be used as a focal point in one of your rooms. Perhaps you think of going to a specialty boutique store in a local mall. You recall the store having poster-sized prints available, rolled up in tubes. You'll have to look for a frame and picture hanging supplies, but you decide the savings would be worth the extra effort. Many of us are bargain shoppers and prefer to shop for decorative items at thrift stores or yard sales. Undoubtedly, some of us will want to display photos of family, friends, or even handcrafted cards given to us by those we love.

Clearly, when it comes to our home, finding decorative items isn't a problem; however, finding decorative items that work within our budget, color scheme, and design motif and express the look and feel of what we want to convey to those who visit can be a challenge. Similarly, finding images for online course design or training projects is not a problem. We have proprietary options for images, such as stock photo sites and subscription services, as well as free resources from the public domain, Creative Commons licenses, and the photos and images we take or create ourselves; however, finding free or affordable images related to our instructional objectives can create a dilemma.

THE SEARCH FOR IMAGES

The filtering options in search engines, while varied, are becoming more and more responsive to user queries. This is helpful because images freely available through the public domain or those that offer a Creative Commons license are not located in any one place, so conducting a keyword search for an image will produce both copyrighted images, images in the public domain, and those with Creative Commons licenses. Fortunately, these images can be filtered from one another. Many search engines have advanced search options; for example, filters for image size, color, or type, such as clip art, photos, and line drawings. Some search engines allow search results to be filtered by license type, as shown in Figure 2.4. Sometimes you can confirm the permissions granted for the use of an image by visiting the site where the image originated. If the permissions are attached to the image, you may be able to access information similar to Figure 2.5 by clicking on the image. If confirmation of permissions isn't readily available, use another image. Even though an image may appear in the search results as being in the public domain or having a Creative Commons license, the image user is responsible for verifying the permissions granted for use of an image. Helpful search terms to get you started include "free public domain images," "free images," and "free photo sharing websites."

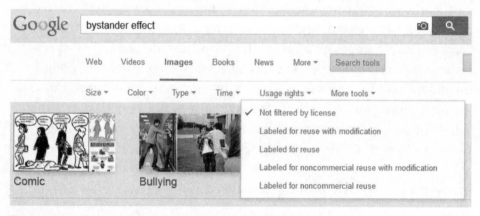

Figure 2.4 Google can filter images by license type

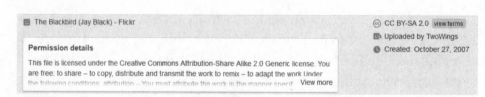

Figure 2.5 A Google image search filtered by the Creative Commons license "labeled for reuse"

DISPLAYING IMAGES IN YOUR COURSE

Let's say you've found lots of images that you have the right to use. How do you go about getting those images into your course? Three skills can be most helpful in displaying images effectively—screen capturing, cropping, and proficient use of a presentation tool.

Screen Capturing Tool

Just as quickly as you can take a selfie or frame a beautiful sunset with your smartphone's camera, screen capturing allows you to quickly take a picture of anything on your computer screen. You can take a screen capture of your desktop, a paused moment from a DVD playing on your computer, or an image displayed through your web browser. When you don't have the ability to download the image to your computer through an icon or printer function, you can use a screen capture, also referred to as a "screenshot," to create a file of the image for later use. One way to capture an image is to the use the "Print Screen" key on your computer keyboard, if available (it may be abbreviated as "Prt Scr" or "Prt Sc"). The print screen function will capture the entire screen or even two screens, if you have dual monitors connected.

Another way to capture an image on your computer is to use a screen capture tool. Screen capture tools may come with your computer's operating system, such as the Window's 7 Snipping Tool. In addition, googling "free screen capture" will return a list of free web tools you can use to capture an image on your screen. Some screen capturing tools will allow you to superimpose text and basic graphics on top of the captured image, as shown in Figure 2.6. This can be helpful when creating tutorials or "how-to" documents. Most of the images throughout this book are screen captures made with various web tools. However, the screen capturing tool I use most is Jing by TechSmith. After downloading the software and creating a free Jing account, here is all you need to do to create a tutorial like the one shown in Figure 2.6:

1. Frame the area you want to capture on your computer.
2. Click the Capture icon.
3. Highlight areas in the screen capture that you want to call attention to using text, color, and basic shapes like arrows and squares.

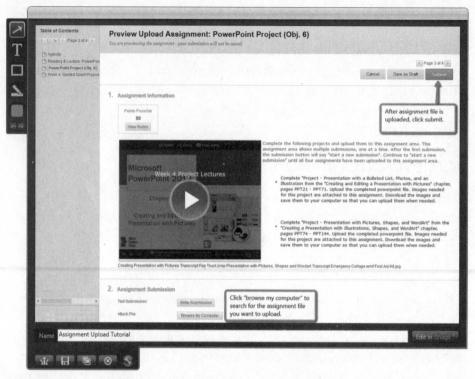

Figure 2.6 The Jing interface showing a screen capture tutorial with superimposed text and shapes

Cropping Tool

If you enjoy scrapbooking hardcopy or digital photos, you are very familiar with the concept of cropping pictures. You can use scissors with a straight line or specialty scissors with scalloped edges to crop a hardcopy photo. You can crop digital photos in heart, diamond, or arrow shapes. Cropping is the act of managing the size, shape, and focal point of an image, as shown in Figure 2.7. Perhaps the focal point of a picture is on the right side of a framed image. Cropping the left side will allow you to remove aspects of the image that are not germane to your topic. In addition, cropping digital images have the added benefit of reducing file size, which can be helpful when upload limits are imposed on your project. Many productivity programs have basic cropping functions that control the size of an image and some productivity programs will crop images into basic shapes like

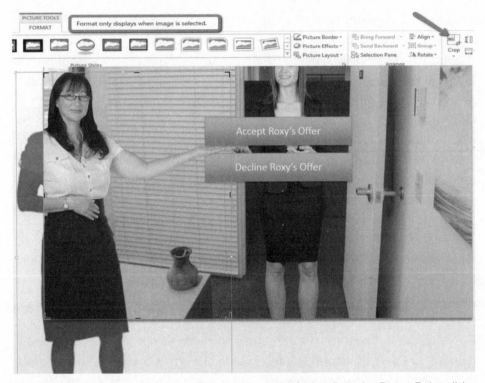

Figure 2.7 The person on the left has been cropped to fit in the PowerPoint slide

circles and hearts. Google "free cropping tool" for a list of free web tools that might be helpful to you. To crop images in any Microsoft office 2013 application:

1. Select the image.
2. Select the crop tool located on the "Picture Tools Format" tab (visible only when the image is selected).
3. Drag the edges of the image to adjust the size and focal point.

Presentation Web Tools

One of the things I really enjoy about our information age is the emphasis on sharing and remixing. Our parents called it repurposing. When you finished eating all the grape jelly from the jar, the jar turned into a drinking glass and had a prominent space in the cabinet, as if it were a colorful tumbler from Tupperware. Our generation heard the "reduce, reuse, recycle" mantra. The large brown paper bags became book covers for school books. My schools required all hardcover books to be covered so that they would be in decent condition for reuse the next year. Similarly, the current generation lives in a sharing and remixing culture. And no, they don't call that plagiarism (that's a discussion for another author).

There are several web tools that facilitate sharing and remixing. What do we mean by that? Most web tools facilitate the sharing of content through links and embed codes, as discussed in the previous chapter. However, it's the remixing that benefits busy content designers. Many web tools facilitate the modification of existing content by allowing their reuse under Creative Commons licensing. For example, Prezi is a popular cloud-based presentation tool. Some Prezi content creators allow their presentations to be copied and modified. Busy designers can use an existing presentation as a template and replace the information with their own. Busy professors can import an existing PowerPoint presentation and add a little Prezi flavor by zooming in on critical information. Without respect to course delivery format, educators at all levels of teaching, borrow ideas from one another and tweak those ideas to make them their own. Web tools facilitate this collegial activity.

Remember, start with what you know. PowerPoint is a powerful presentation tool; it has been the classroom teacher's best friend for decades. Many web tools make it possible to use PowerPoint presentations that you've previously created or have been given by the publisher of a textbook. A presentation tool I've used and recommended to faculty is Brainshark. Figure 2.8 is a screenshot of an embedded lecture built for Dr. Elaine Ahumada, associate professor of public administration, chair of history and government, and director of master's in public administration at the Online and Professional Studies Division of California Baptist University. Because PowerPoint files with audio can be quite large, Dr. Ahumada uploaded the PowerPoint presentation file and audio file separately. Together we repurposed her PowerPoint presentation with the separate audio file and merged them into one presentation. The free version of the Brainshark web tool accepts PowerPoint files, allows you

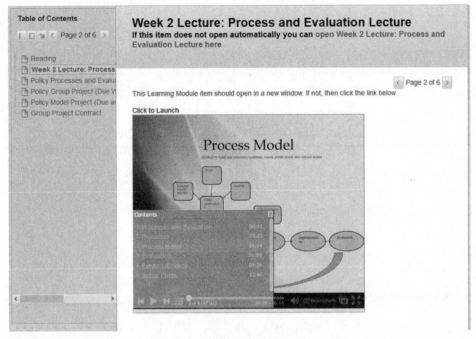

Figure 2.8 Instructor PowerPoint file repurposed in a web tool with an embed code to integrate into a content item of an LMS

Image courtesy of Dr. Elaine Ahumada from California Baptist University's Online and Professional Studies

to narrate each slide or upload an audio file, and presents the viewer of the Brainshark presentation with a table of contents from which to navigate the presentation nonsequentially, as shown in Figure 2.8. Because students can hear the instructor deliver the content, the instructor's presence is felt in the online environment. After creating the free Brainshark account:

1. Upload a PowerPoint file to Brainshark.

2. Add audio, or record using a microphone.

3. End the session when you have completed the narration for each slide.

4. Copy the link and the embed code to share the presentation in your course.

BEST USES FOR IMAGES

Thinking back to our new home example, once we acquire the images, we use them to convey elements of our personality. Typically we want a welcoming feel for the living room. The family room typically displays pictures of those who live in the home along with pictures of close friends and relatives. Similarly, your online course can use images to create instructional diagrams, tutorials, and course themes, and to showcase student-created images. As the designer or instructor, you don't have to provide every image. Consider designing assignments and icebreakers that encourage students to contribute images to the course.

IMAGES TO MOTIVATE AND ENCOURAGE

The students in most courses span the continuum of cognitive ability, discipline specific experiences, skills in the primary language of instruction, reasons for taking the course, and motivation to complete the course—just to name a few variables. How can diverse students in the same course be encouraged to participate at high levels? Because instructors and students are separated by distance and time in an online course, the visual cues students get from peers and the instructor that say their contributions are valued are not readily apparent.

To meet this need, Dr. Riste Simnjanovski, the assistant academic dean at the Online and Professional Studies Division of California Baptist University, created and piloted the use of digital badges in his online courses. Digital badges are a type of currency that can be earned throughout his course. Students can choose to display the badges in the online course or on their personal website by uploading the badge to a service that supports digital badges, such Mozilla's OpenBadges site. Additionally, Dr. Simnjanovski uses "hidden badges" to motivate exceptional students. For example, he e-mailed a student to privately award a badge for earning a score in the top 5 percent of the class. While the awards were made privately through e-mail, Dr. Simnjanovski received several e-mail inquiries

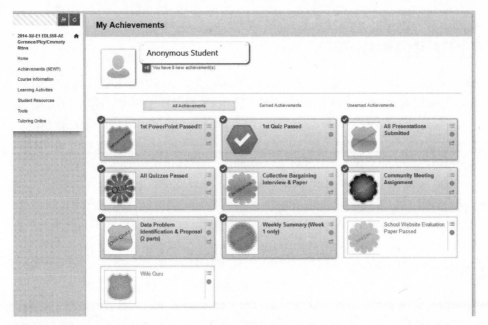

Figure 2.9 Images used as digital badges to acknowledge exceptional work in the online environment

Image of courtesy of Dr. Riste Simnjanovski from California Baptist University's Online and Professional Studies

from students asking what these hidden badges were and how they could earn them. Such motivators are not typically associated with adult learners. However, Dr. Simnjanovski believes they contribute to the increase in student effort and assignment quality. Criteria for badges are at the instructor's discretion and can be directly connected to course objectives. The badges shown in Figure 2.9 were created using images from a Google search, Flickr, and similar graphics applications. Some of the badges used in Figure 2.9 were created using Webestools, a web 2.0 badge generator. Once you create the images and save them on your computer, you can copy them onto a student's submitted assignment along with your assignment feedback. Because Blackboard has an achievement module, Dr. Simnjanovski uploaded the images to it and created rules that release the badges to students when the criteria are met.

CREATE A WELCOMING COURSE ENVIRONMENT

Have you heard the adage that people don't care how much you know, until they know how much you care? Assuming this is true, what feeling tone do you want to convey when students enter your course? How can the content pages throughout the course display hospitality? Page banners and themed icons are great starting points for creating a welcoming environment.

Just as realtors announce an open house by placing a sign in the front yard of a home for sale, banners in an online course visually confirm that learners have arrived at the correct location. Sometimes publishers include a banner image with an online course cartridge for the more popular learning management systems, like Blackboard. You can also use free web tools to create banners and other images, as shown in Figure 2.10. Google "free graphic web tools" and the search will return several graphic design sites, many of which are template driven, so that you can create a

Figure 2.10 A course banner, for an online teaching and learning course, created using free graphics and the drag-and-drop features of the Canva web tool

professional banner or image for your course homepage without graphic design experience. The banner in Figure 2.10 was created using Canva, a free web tool that offers drag-and-drop design templates. The laptop, iPhone, and iPad in the figure were free graphics provided through Canva. The images displayed through the free graphics are screenshots from previously taught courses that were uploaded, dragged, and dropped into the free graphics. After you arrive at the Canva.com homepage and create a free account, follow these steps:

1. Select a design template.

2. Drag and drop an image onto the template.

3. Modify text and images as desired.

4. Save and download the image to use as needed.

VISUAL CUES

Think about all the visual cues you observe every day to let you know the behavioral expectation of a particular situation—the signs on the road, or the indicator lights at available checkout stands in the grocery store. Icons can help students understand which items in the course are for reading versus items that require a response. Learning management systems may use icons by default, whereas you may need to add your own icons to website templates used for a course or training online. Matthew Acevedo, an instructional designer with Florida International University Online, creates his own icons to enhance student recognition of the various types of instructional content in a course. Figure 2.11 shows icons that help users distinguish content for viewing, reading, discussing, or doing. The visual cues also help students find what they need when they need it by reducing their dependency on text.

Acevedo used a freely licensed icon set to develop a set of headers and content-type icons that can be consistently used throughout a course. The Entypo Pictogram Suite is an example of a freely licensed set of icons that can be extracted and manipulated using photo editing software. He created header images for course sections such as "Directions" and "Resources" and used specific icons in numbered or bulleted lists for student directions.

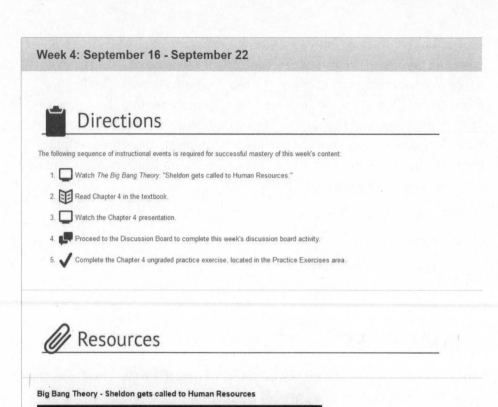

Week 4: September 16 - September 22

Directions

The following sequence of instructional events is required for successful mastery of this week's content:

1. Watch *The Big Bang Theory*: "Sheldon gets called to Human Resources."
2. Read Chapter 4 in the textbook.
3. Watch the Chapter 4 presentation.
4. Proceed to the Discussion Board to complete this week's discussion board activity.
5. Complete the Chapter 4 ungraded practice exercise, located in the Practice Exercises area.

Resources

Big Bang Theory - Sheldon gets called to Human Resources

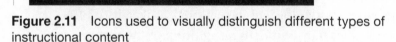

Figure 2.11 Icons used to visually distinguish different types of instructional content

Image courtesy of Matthew Acevedo from Florida International University Online

CONSISTENT TYPES OF CONTENT

Brain-based learning research tells us that the human brain is a meaning-making organism (Bor, 2012). While the new and the novel create interest, predictable patterns create comfort. Given the physical absence of a facilitator, online courses need a healthy mix of both. When you walk into your neighborhood grocery store, you are comforted by knowing that produce can be found to the left when you enter the store. However, you

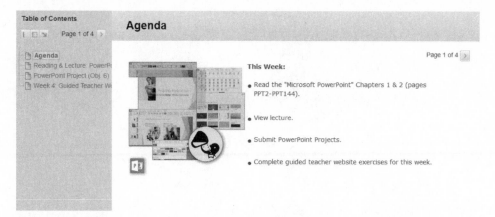

Figure 2.12 First content page in each of eight learning modules begins with the week's agenda

hope to see a variety of produce in this area. And your culinary palate is piqued by the unexpected find of a guacamole seasoning packet by the avocados. Similarly, students will find comfort in knowing that the first content page of a learning module contains the instructor's expectations for the unit, such as those shown in Figure 2.12. Predictable content items support learners' self-efficacy as they navigate the online environment. For example, a series of learning modules that contain an overview, a lecture, a discussion, and an assignment orient students to the location of instructional materials. In the absence of a face-to-face instructor, students need to know where to find what they need when they need it. While it is important to provide predictable content items in a particular order to support learners in the online environment, everything doesn't have to be the same. The instructor or a guest speaker can narrate lecture content. Narrated and embedded student presentations can provide instructional content. Discussions can be centered around questions, video content, or images. Assignments can be project or problem based, oral or written.

In a professional development course delivered through a blended format, Dr. Wendi Kappers, a network engineer and instructional designer, and Sara Ombres, an instructional designer and educational technologist, provided participants with "Blended Course Design Tips." A written reflection is used repeatedly throughout the course in the blog tool to remind participants to consider the real-world connections to course material. A Blog icon serves as a visual reminder that the written reflection takes place

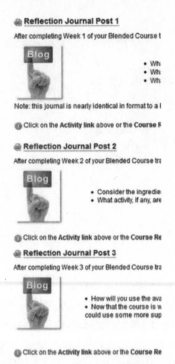

Reflection Journal Post 1

After completing Week 1 of your Blended Course t

Blog

- Wh
- Wh
- Wh

Note: this journal is nearly identical in format to a l

Click on the **Activity link** above or the **Course F**

Reflection Journal Post 2

After completing Week 2 of your Blended Course tra

Blog

- Consider the ingredie
- What activity, if any, are

Click on the **Activity link** above or the **Course Re**

Reflection Journal Post 3

After completing Week 3 of your Blended Course tra

Blog

- How will you use the ava
- Now that the course is w
  could use some more sup

Click on the **Activity link** above or the **Course Re**

Figure 2.13   Repeated content elements are enhanced by visual cues
Image courtesy of Dr. Wendi Kappers and Sara Ombres from Embry-Riddle Aeronautical University Worldwide Campus

in that specific location in the course. Figure 2.13 shows how repeated content elements are enhanced by visual cues.

ESTABLISH A POSITIVE LEARNING COMMUNITY

When my kids were in preschool through primary grades, my husband and I moved the family into a newly built residential single family home community. Most of the families that moved in around the same time had kids ranging from infants to about middle school age, and most of the kids played together in the neighborhood. This was back in the day when kids still rode bikes and scooters and played games in the street. After we had lived in our new home for several months, our five-year-old neighbor knocked on the door. From the family room my husband and I simply yelled, "Come on in, the door's unlocked." In walked our little neighbor. Without a greeting or a smile, she looked at me and my husband and simply went upstairs where our kids were hanging out. She didn't say hello or, "Where are Brittany, LaNyce, and Craig?" or, "May I go upstairs?" My husband and I laughed with each other, with that "I thought we owned this house" look on our faces.

As I relive that moment, I feel honored that a five-year-old child felt comfortable enough to walk into our home as if she lived there every day. I feel honored that her parents felt a part of our family community enough to allow their five-year-old to walk into our home on her own. Similarly, students enrolled in an online course or training make up a learning community. They become a learning community simply by membership in your course and the fact that they will share similar experiences throughout the duration of the course. If left to chance, however, the likelihood that the online learning community will be a positive influence on its members is significantly diminished. Creating a positive learning community begins by helping students connect with one another beyond name, major, and year in school. Images can be used to evoke laughter, smiles, and empathy through common experiences and feelings.

Just as your home or office may have a space dedicated to pictures of your family and friends, there are a myriad of ways to share your personality with students and allow them to do so with you and one another. Course introductions are one way to do this. Instructors may use the discussion forum space to type a brief academic history of themselves and then allow students to share information about academic majors and future goals. While this may be interesting information, students will already have a significant amount of required reading. Will they want to read mini biographies for the fifteen to thirty individuals in a course? What we really want to do with course introductions is engage the affective domain with "laugh out loud," "hmmm," or "aha!" moments.

One semester, I tried a different approach to the course introductions. I asked students to upload their favorite meme and explain why it was their favorite. I modeled the expectation by posting and explaining my favorite meme. Figure 2.14 shows an original meme created by a student from a home photo. Don't the puppy-dog eyes just make you smile? Or maybe smirk and shake your head? Others found memes online that they enjoyed. This was the first time 100 percent of my students participated in the online course introductions. One student responded in a letter

Figure 2.14 Student-created meme from a home photo submitted to the blog space for course introductions

that she really liked the meme introductions because it was fun to see her classmates' meme choices and even more fun to see the instructor's choice. Through this activity, students also have the opportunity to contribute to the look and feel of the course. The introduction in Figure 2.14 used the blog tool; Figure 2.15 uses the discussion board tool for course introductions.

IMAGES TO SHOWCASE LESSON OBJECTIVES AND LEARNING OUTCOMES

Just as a dentist may have framed images of smiling people with perfectly aligned white teeth on the walls of the examining room, or a cardiologist with a framed, labeled diagram of the heart, images can be both decorative and relevant to course learning outcomes. How can the access page

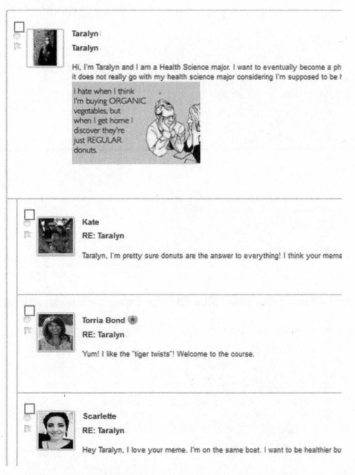

Figure 2.15 Discussion board tool used for student meme submissions—peer responses to the student's meme were not solicited or required

to learning modules be designed to reinforce the topic of study? Jan G. Neal, lead instructional designer for doctoral studies for Embry-Riddle University in Daytona Beach, Florida, uses images to introduce students to seminal contributors in the discipline while also introducing them to module topics. Providing a list of activities is one way to make the organizational structure of the module apparent. Module graphics should add value, not just glamour, and prose should be meaningful and succinct. The module splash page in Figure 2.16 shows images of pioneering

Figure 2.16 Splash page to learning module displays images of a seminal contributors and copyright permissions from the alt text field

Image courtesy of Jan Neal from Embry-Riddle Aeronautical University Worldwide Campus

researchers with a relevant quote, intended to both engage students and inform them about seminal contributors to the field of human-centered design. In addition, the alt text describes the photo and it's copyright information, which is used by screen readers to describe images to blind learners. The list of activities next to the image serves as a table of contents or advanced organizer for students. To create something similar:

1. Identify the pioneers or primary contributors to the field. Find pictures of them that you can use and adapt either with permission or through the appropriate Creative Commons license.

2. Using photo editing software or a presentation tool similar to PowerPoint, modify the images by replacing the background with a neutral or noncontrasting color and resizing as needed, then add a relevant quote (such as an assertion or question) by that person that encapsulates the module topic or chief idea.

3. Embed the image and include an appropriate attribution, either under the image or in the hover or rollover alt text.

4. Add the module activities to the right of the image. To keep the activities list adjacent to the image regardless of how the web page is reflowed when resized by the user, use a table that has one row with two columns, as shown in Figure 2.16.

INCORPORATING VIDEO IN ONLINE INSTRUCTION

The value of video to spark interest, stimulate dialogue, and bring real-world applications to the classroom has long been appreciated. The use of video integration for teaching and training online is growing, enabled by many learning management systems through the use of "mashups"—a combination of data sources presented to users in a unique web context. For example, Figure 2.17 shows several mashup options that integrate in the text editor of Blackboard Learn. Mashups make it easier to search video and image repositories and integrate them in online courses or trainings. However, not all learning management systems or website text editors have this functionality, so you need to find a video sharing site to host the videos you create, so you can integrate them into a learning management system or website. With the proliferation of free web tools and social media, everyone can create multimedia content and make it available to anyone around the world.

Figure 2.17 Instructor-created lecture uploaded to YouTube and embedded in Blackboard using the mashup feature

Image courtesy of Dr. Elizabeth Morris from California Baptist University's Online and Professional Studies

VIDEO HOSTING

Before you begin creating videos for your course, you should consider identifying a free video hosting and sharing site. Hosting video on the Web ensures that students can access your videos wherever internet access is available, using the variety of computers and mobile devices on the market. In addition, viewing videos directly from the Web spares students the long download times and other technical issues related to uploaded video versus streamed video. Dr. Elizabeth Morris, associate dean for the Online and Professional Studies Division of California Baptist University, hosts algebra lectures she creates on YouTube. Figure 2.18 shows how the mashup feature in Blackboard is used to embed the video lecture into the content page, after being uploaded to her YouTube account. A Google search using the terms "video hosting" will present several options for hosting the videos you create.

A video hosting site allows individuals to upload original videos, share videos with others, comment on videos, and search for video content. Many sites allow the sharing of videos through links and embed codes. With these, videos can be shared on websites and in an LMS. To ensure that you respect a video creator's copyright, use videos within the functionality available through the video hosting site or within the parameters of the listed copyright license.

SCREENCASTING

Screencasting is the act of recording moving actions on your computer screen. It's a basic skill needed for instructors and trainers to create their own videos. A Google search for "free screencasting tools" will return a results page with many options. Choose a free screencasting tool with the following features:

- The option to narrate while recording your computer screen
- The option to display a picture of yourself as you record and narrate
- Rendering of MP4 video files, the most flexible file format for video
- Several methods of sharing or saving the finished file

Screencasting presentations facilitate the instructor's presence in an online course or training, so you want a screencasting tool that allows your voice to be heard and your face to be seen. Some free tools do not

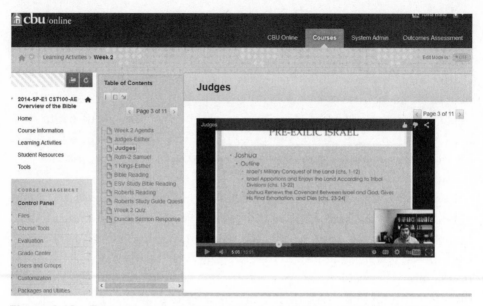

Figure 2.18 Free web tool used to screencast an instructor's PowerPoint presentation, upload to a video sharing site, and embed in Blackboard

Image courtesy of Dr. Matthew Emerson from California Baptist University's Online and Professional Studies

render screencasted videos in MP4 format, a versatile format for uploading to video hosting sites, social media sites, blogs, and course management systems. Many sites will offer seamless uploading of screencasted videos to video hosting or social media sites. With a little experimentation, finding a free screencasting tool with features that work for you will encourage you to infuse instructor-created videos into your course.

Once you find a screencasting tool that you're comfortable using, you'll find a number of ways to support learners through screencasted materials. Dr. Matthew Emerson, assistant professor of Christian ministries and chair of arts and sciences at the Online and Professional Studies Division of California Baptist University, narrates his PowerPoint presentation for students, as shown in Figure 2.18. Instructors can also create a course orientation video that shows students how to navigate the course management system. Instructors might consider screencasting a review of the course syllabus and learning outcomes. Screencasting makes it possible to model and explain assignment expectations. It is one way to make sure that learners have the information and resources they need when they need it. To create a similar screencast:

1. Navigate to your favorite screencasting tool in your preferred web browser. Dr. Emerson used Screencast-O-Matic (screencast-o -matic.com)

2. Select a previously created PowerPoint presentation.

3. Shape the screencast tool's borders around the edges of your slide. Be ready to use the arrows or scroll bar to advance slides during the screencast.

4. Test your microphone and turn on your webcam (if that functionality is available).

5. Narrate your presentation.

6. Save the presentation to your computer or upload directly to You-Tube (if that functionality is available).

DISPLAYING VIDEO

There are three possibilities for displaying video on a content page. Common ways of accessing video from a content page include creating hyperlinked text on the content page that takes the student to the video when they click on the text as seen in Figure 2.19. This is more convenient for students than copying the video URL onto the content page, which forces them to copy the link into a browser window. This can be frustrating if they don't copy and paste the link accurately. A second method is to hyperlink an uploaded image or icon, so a click on the image or icon takes the student to the video. This was shown in Figure 1.10 in the Chapter One discussion of linking to content—a skill used to keep course design L.I.T.E. The image of the PowerPoint slide in Figure 1.10 was linked to external content.

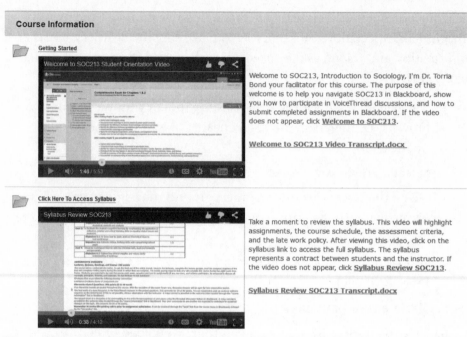

Figure 2.19 Embedded and active text-linked videos with uploaded transcript files for accessibility

Figure 2.19 shows two videos embedded in the content page, with links to the video on the video hosting site, as well as a video transcript for full accessibility to students. Given the changes in web browser security and the compatibility of those security features with LMSs, it's a good practice to embed video with an active link to the video just in case browser security prevents the video from displaying. It's even a better practice to create the active links with the specific name of the video so that users of screen readers or other assistive technologies will *hear* the specific name of the link, not a vague reference such as "click here."

Yet another way is to embed the video directly on the page using the embed code discussed in Chapter One. When displaying a series of videos in the same content space, consider creating a playlist. This allows you to embed one video frame and have all videos in the series play in succession as seen in Figure 2.20. These techniques work equally well to display podcasts or interactive web pages in your course.

Figure 2.20 YouTube playlist makes multiple videos accessible from the same location while minimizing the number of content items
Image courtesy of Courtney Lloyd, adjunct professor for American Sign Language

A VIDEO-BASED DISCUSSION FORUM

Once you've established a free account with a video hosting service and learned to link or embed videos into an LMS or website, you are ready to explore creative uses for video as an instructional tool. Dr. Yvonne Thai, assistant professor and lead faculty for sociology at the Online and Professional Studies Division of California Baptist University, has used videos to provide context to discussion questions. Figure 2.21 shows the use of the YouTube mashup in Blackboard's text editor to embed a video in a discussion forum. The questions posed to students represent the various levels of Bloom's Taxonomy, a classification schema that identifies lower- and higher-level thinking questions. By asking students comprehension questions, you can determine whether they understand the context of the video before you ask them to apply their understanding to a new context. These steps will help you prepare for a video-based online discussion:

1. Locate a short video on a controversial topic in your field.

2. Embed the video in the discussion board area.

3. Propose questions with many correct possibilities.

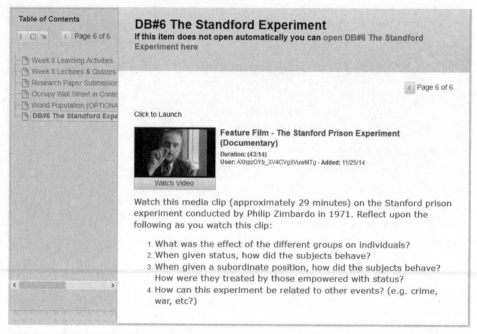

DB#6 The Standford Experiment
If this item does not open automatically you can open DB#6 The Standford Experiment here

< Page 6 of 6

Click to Launch

Feature Film - The Stanford Prison Experiment (Documentary)
Duration: (43:14)
User: AXhpzOYb_XV4CVgXVuwMTg - Added: 11/25/14

Watch Video

Watch this media clip (approximately 29 minutes) on the Stanford prison experiment conducted by Philip Zimbardo in 1971. Reflect upon the following as you watch this clip:

1. What was the effect of the different groups on individuals?
2. When given status, how did the subjects behave?
3. When given a subordinate position, how did the subjects behave? How were they treated by those empowered with status?
4. How can this experiment be related to other events? (e.g. crime, war, etc?)

Figure 2.21   Video-based discussion forums with comprehension and higher-order thinking questions

Image courtesy of Dr. Yvonne Thai of California Baptist University's Online and Professional Studies Division

SUMMARY

With the understanding that copyright laws are intended to ensure that authors maintain control of their intellectual property, I suggested two guiding principles. Treating others the way you would want to be treated and considering the interests of others can potentially prevent copyright infringement. While copyright laws are intended to ensure authors are allowed to benefit from their intellectual property, fair use laws allow the public to engage in discourse about copyrighted works. The TEACH Act ensures that educational and government institutions do not unfairly copy, reproduce, or distribute copyrighted works. Images from the public domain and those with Creative Commons licenses are available from free photo sharing and image sites.

The skills most useful to learn for customizing the arrangement of images on the content page of an LMS or website template include cropping, screen capture, and use of presentation software with templates. Video hosting sites are a good source of content and provide the means by which to share videos through hyperlinks and embed codes. Screencasting was introduced as a way to create instructor videos for the purpose of narrating PowerPoint presentations, demonstrating course navigation, and reviewing a course syllabus. Multimedia integration provides many opportunities to accommodate varied learning styles, increase student engagement, and support learner navigation of the online course.

WHAT'S NEXT?

1. Explore your organization's documented policy about copyrighted materials and their inclusion in your online course or training.

2. Search for pictures that illustrate concepts you plan to discuss in your course, and confirm the copyright permissions that allow their use in your organizations authentication required secure portal.

3. Visit the Creative Commons website. Familiarize yourself with the symbols associated with different types of licenses. Locate multimedia displaying Creative Commons license that can be used in your online course or training.

4. Find or create a banner that depicts a central concept in a course you are planning. Upload it to a course you are designing.

5. Design a course introduction that allows students to express themselves with images. Build the course introduction into the course you are designing.

6. Find or create themed icons for the different types of activities in the course you are designing. Google "free icons" for a list of sites to get you started. Upload them to your course.

7. Screencast a course orientation and upload it to a video hosting site that provides an embed code and a link you can use to integrate the content with an LMS or website.

3

HOW DO I FACILITATE INSTRUCTION AND INTERACTION?

Design is the conscious effort to impose a meaningful order.
—Victor Papanek

Lesson planning is one of the most creative activities in which instructors engage. How it's done is influenced by philosophical beliefs about teaching; how students learn; whether you are teaching concepts, skills, or affective dispositions; and whether or not prerequisite knowledge is required, among other factors (Armstrong, Henson, & Savage, 2009; Ornstein & Hunkins, 2009). Most educational and training practitioners would agree that constructing a lesson begins with learning outcomes, lesson objectives, and a plan for assessment, all of which are aligned with the instructional procedures, information, and resources provided (Ornstein & Hunkins, 2009). Many of us will outline units of instruction to correspond with chapters in the textbook. Some may choose to design instruction topically based on current issues in the field. Others may design instruction around experiential activities that serve as a common reference point, with lesson content focused on exploring essential questions in the discipline. Still others may design instruction around the performance of specific skills. The beauty of visually designing instruction is that there are many right ways to do it, as long as the learning outcomes, objectives, assessment measures, and instructional procedures, information, and resources are aligned. This chapter explores the impact of pedagogical practices for facilitating online discussions, student collaboration, and educational models of instruction on the visual design of an online course.

HOW CAN I FACILITATE ONLINE DISCUSSIONS?

Providing opportunities for asynchronous and synchronous communication between learners in the course is an important part of creating a sense of presence and building a learning community in an online course. Learning to work with others across time and distance is a new skill for many taking online courses. Although learners may use social media to communicate with family and friends who are not in close proximity, they are not always cognizant of how to do this for academic purposes. Therefore the skill of interacting and collaborating with peers online must be taught and purposefully planned by the instructor.

The concepts of "interaction" and "collaboration" are occasionally used synonymously by instructors and trainers. However, they are distinct and separate pedagogical strategies. Interaction includes opportunities to share and discuss content. Collaboration is the sharing and discussing of content for the purpose of producing a shared product such as a presentation or project (Horton, 2012). Because interaction and collaboration involve sharing and discussing content, consider having students upload pictures of themselves that appear whenever they post a comment. This helps to personalize the online interaction and collaboration experience, particularly when working in small groups. In addition, clearly defining the parameters for interaction and collaboration is foundational for a positive experience, and for valid assessment information that influences instruction. Interaction and collaboration are essential elements in developing and sustaining a learning community.

As instructors, we want to foster dynamic conversations around course content. We want our students to reflect deeply on meaningful questions and contribute responses that encourage their peers to do the same. Sometimes learners have a difficult time providing thoughtful responses and commenting critically to their peers. Responses that begin with, "I think . . ." and comments to peers that simply say, "I agree" tend to make us feel as though online discussions can never be as robust as face-to-face classroom discussions. The desire to foster dynamic conversations prompted me to take the Online Learning Consortium's one-week online workshop, "Successful Online Outcomes: Improved Discussions." I learned that shallow student responses were in part due to the discussion forum not being set up to follow the common courtesies of face-to-face conversations. For example, a classroom discussion in which everyone is talking at once is no more productive than a discussion forum where everyone creates their own thread on the same topic. In both instances, the discussion lacks focus, and individual participants are not able to display the common courtesy of listening attentively. Another example would be the rude behavior of walking out on a speaker. When a peer is making a presentation in front of the class, most students would wait until the presentation has ended before standing and leaving the room. Similarly, when you don't know when members of an asynchronous online discussion are coming and going, participants are left to wonder whether anyone cares enough to read what was posted, especially if it never gets a response. The following sections emphasize the system settings that can be applied to create the visual design of a discussion forum that simulates the flow of a face-to-face conversation.

Allow Students to Self-Enroll in a Small Discussion Group

If you've ever taken a massive open online course (MOOC), you know that there can be hundreds or even thousands of individuals in the course. It's impossible to read everyone's self-introduction, let alone their contributions to discussion forums. By creating small group spaces online, reading discussion comments becomes more manageable. Discussion group size depends on the task at hand. Based on personal experiences as an instructor and online student, a collaborative project discussion of three to five active members is manageable. For brainstorming and generating ideas, groups of ten can be appropriate. Beyond ten active members in a group, it may be difficult for each member to consider what everyone has posted. If a student doesn't voluntarily sign up for a group, no one else is affected, and the instructor can work with those students separately. What if a group member goes MIA after signing up for a group? That depends on the nature of the group task. For cooperative tasks, if students divide responsibilities to complete separately, they will hurt the scores of active members. However, collaborative tasks will not negatively impact active group members because the contributions of a group member are dependent on the whole group, not just one member doing their part. The distinction between these assignment types will be discussed later.

Make Groups Available Based on Available Study Time

Most students have a less-than-positive experience with group assignments. Even though the ability to effectively work in teams is among the top three skills wanted by employers, most students approach the group assignment experience with anxiety. In a study of student attitudes toward group work conducted by Gottschall and Garcia-Bayonas (2008), 1,249 undergraduate education, business administration, and mathematics majors were surveyed on perceived benefits and challenges of working in groups. Students surveyed identified two positive and two negative aspects of working in groups. On the one hand, students acknowledge it's important to learn to work with others and that more ideas can be generated by a group than an individual. On the other hand, students find it difficult to coordinate schedules, and they resent "freeloaders" earning the same high grade as those who participate and complete group tasks.

It's difficult to have a thoughtful asynchronous discussion when one group member tends to post comments at the beginning of the week and another group member doesn't even log into the course until the end of the week. One solution is to allow students to choose a group based on time periods. For example, create a couple of Monday through Wednesday groups and Friday through Sunday groups. Set one of the Monday through Wednesday groups for students who plan to access the course during the business day and the other after the business day. Over time, and with student feedback, you'll figure out the popular times when students access the course and can create groups accordingly. This addresses the difficulty of coordinating schedules identified by students in the Gottschall and Garcia-Bayonas study. By allowing students to self-enroll in groups based on available study time, students are voluntarily subscribing to a group norm for discussion. This commitment to work with others whose study times for interaction are compatible encourages frequent engagement in the discussion forum during the group availability. This norm can be reinforced by the instructor's late policy if necessary. Another strategy is to allow discussions to take place over two weeks. This allows all students one week to post a response and another week to review the responses and make comments. Lastly, if your LMS permits the instructor to allow students to subscribe to a forum, use the subscription feature to allow students to receive e-mail notifications when members of their group post to the forum. This will facilitate timely responses to group member's contributions to the discussion.

Teach Students How to Collaborate Online

At the time of this writing, online learning is still a relatively new format. Even for students who are comfortable learning online, collaborating with peers is a learned skill that needs to be taught—if for no other reason than to explain the specific collaboration tools in the context of your course and the assignment. Just as you would create a course tour to orient individual students to the online course environment, the same orientation is needed for the group space, identifying what tools are available in the group space and how they should be used in the context of the group project.

Give Each Discussion Forum a Headline

If you shop regularly at commercial grocery stores, I'm sure you've noticed the headlines of magazines and tabloids at the checkout counter. On the Web, headlines are used in articles by freelance writers and bloggers to create interest. If you're just standing in line waiting for the person in front of you to pay for their groceries and get them bagged, you've probably picked up a magazine because you were enticed by the headline. Writers and bloggers recognize that the headline is the first phrase encountered

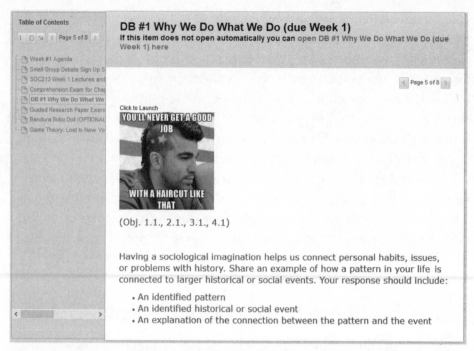

Figure 3.1 A titled discussion forum with a relevant image used as the discussion entry point along with response criteria

by the reader, and the goal is to make them stop clicking around and read the entire piece. Using an intriguing headline for a discussion forum title can generate more interest in a topic than the title "Discussion Board #1." Figure 3.1 shows a titled discussion forum with a relevant image used as the entry point into the discussion forum. If the discussion forum headline draws the student in and the accompanying image is controversial, critical engagement is more likely to follow.

Consider Turning Off Permissions to Create New Threads

Threads represent separate discussions. Allowing students to create new threads when you want them to respond to a specific question you've asked causes related comments to be missed or buried in an excessive number of disconnected threads. Turning off the creation of new threads using the discussion forum settings in the LMS forces students to enter the thread and simply reply to the original posts and the responses of peers. In this way, the conversation stays in the same thread.

Use a Discussion Rubric or Checklist to Evaluate Participation

Rubrics and checklists are great tools for communicating assignment expectations. Rubrics can be holistic, resulting in a single score based on the whole of a submission, or analytic, resulting in a score for each of several criteria. Rubrics have two benefits for instructors. First, they can be used as a quality assurance check for instructors to confirm that objectives, instruction, and resources are in alignment. The process of writing the descriptive language for each level of performance for a specific criteria helps instructors ensure that students are being assessed on lesson objectives for which instruction and resources were provided. While the writing of language for levels of performance for each criteria is initially time intensive, the student benefits from the clarity of the assignment expectations, and the instructor is focused on the elements that demonstrate achievement. Second, rubrics save time during assignment evaluation. If the rubric language is written well, the need for individual comments on assignments is minimized and students know what they need to do to revise the assignment or to improve on the next assignment. I've been asked whether I use rubrics for everything or just for major assignments. For the reasons stated, I proudly wave the flag that says I use rubrics for absolutely everything, even if it's five points for a self-introduction or extra credit assignment. Communicating assignment expectations is critically important. Discussion assignments are not created just for something to do. They are integrated into the course learning outcomes, and student discussion responses are assessed for specific lesson objectives. Although I use a rubric for everything, those rubrics are not always extensive analytic rubrics. For simple assignments they are more holistic and may be communicated to students through a checklist like the following one posted to the instructional page:

SAMPLE CHECKLIST COMMUNICATING EXPECTATIONS FOR A DISCUSSION ASSIGNMENT

Your comments to two peers should include one of the following:

- Share and/or compare a connection with a peer's response.
- Explore a difference of opinion related to a peer's response.
- Exchange resources and information related to a peer's response.
- Generate a solution to a problem related to a peer's response.

Your comments to peers should have the following effect on the discussion:

- Broaden the scope of the discussion.
- Reference assigned readings or other resources.
- Communicate respectfully with those who express dissenting views.
- Promote sustained dialogue with peers.
- Demonstrate ability to provide feedback to peers.

PLANNING GROUP PROJECTS ONLINE

Facilitating group projects builds on this same structure by adding two pedagogical strategies to the discussion's organizational structure: the use of collaborative assignments and the strategy of scaffolding the assignment throughout the course. When there's a paycheck in the balance, employees find a way to complete group tasks. However, when it's just a matter of a grade for an assignment, the motivation to find time to collaborate with group members varies among students. As a result, most students bemoan group assignments because nonparticipating group members tend to earn the same grade as those who fully participate and complete the project. Or the whole group is penalized because one group member doesn't complete the part of the project agreed upon (Gottschall & Garcia-Bayonas, 2008). Developing collaborative assignments and scaffolding those assignments throughout the course can significantly minimize the negative experiences associated with group projects online.

Assignments that allow group members to divide responsibilities and complete them independently leave room for a nonparticipating group member to benefit from the work of those who participate. In contrast, collaborative assignments require all group members to work toward a single shared product through consensus. To reach a consensus, the group needs to generate ideas to discuss. Consider requiring every group member to post ideas and suggestions. From the ideas and suggestions contributed, discussion ensues until consensus is reached; then any group member can summarize the group's final decision. If a group member chooses not to participate, the rest of the group can still proceed with the discussion of the ideas and suggestions presented. How is this reflected in the grading? A rubric is used to evaluate each group member's individual response (Figure 3.2). The rubric achievement criteria include participating in the agreed-upon window for collaboration and the posting of the group's consensus. Group members who don't post ideas or suggestions will fail the assignment. Conversely, if all group members post ideas and suggestions, but no one remembers to post the groups consensus, it is not possible to fail the assignment. In short accelerated courses, there is no time to wait for a group leader to emerge or to hope there is an organizer in the group who knows how to encourage their peers to begin talking online. It's more efficient for the instructor to build the brainstorming processes through *scaffolding* the assignment.

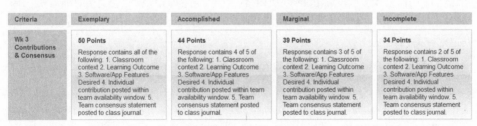

Criteria	Exemplary	Accomplished	Marginal	Incomplete
Wk 3 Contributions & Consensus	**50 Points** Response contains all of the following: 1. Classroom context 2. Learning Outcome 3. Software/App Features Desired 4. Individual contribution posted within team availability window. 5. Team consensus statement posted to class journal.	**44 Points** Response contains 4 of 5 of the following: 1. Classroom context 2. Learning Outcome 3. Software/App Features Desired 4. Individual contribution posted within team availability window. 5. Team consensus statement posted to class journal.	**39 Points** Response contains 3 of 5 of the following: 1. Classroom context 2. Learning Outcome 3. Software/App Features Desired 4. Individual contribution posted within team availability window. 5. Team consensus statement posted to class journal.	**34 Points** Response contains 2 of 5 of the following: 1. Classroom context 2. Learning Outcome 3. Software/App Features Desired 4. Individual contribution posted within team availability window. 5. Team consensus statement posted to class journal.

Figure 3.2   One way to hold learners accountable for contributing to the group

Scaffold Multifaceted Projects

Scaffolding an assignment involves dividing large tasks into incremental steps, preferably with explanations and models of success. In doing this, instructors help students manage their time with respect to the length of the course and to complete project tasks in small incremental steps. To scaffold a large assignment, instructors might consider the following:

1. Identify the steps required to complete the assignment. Divide multistep projects into small incremental tasks that are distributed across the length of the course. For example, if the project is to be completed by the last week of an eight-week course, you might divide the project into five incremental tasks. Figure 3.3 shows the first of four steps in a team grant proposal project. The graphic is of the first slide of the instructions for the project and links to resources to complete the first step.

2. Provide each group with space for brainstorming and recording group consensus. Don't leave it up to the group members to find a place to meet virtually. The small group discussion can take place in discussion forums, blog spaces, or wiki spaces. Set up one location for group members to meet and discuss. Figure 3.4 shows the discussion forum used for collaboration.

3. Prepare the group space for brainstorming. Consider the decisions that group members must agree upon, and create spaces for those specific discussions. Figure 3.4 also shows the decisions that must be made for successful completion of the grant. Notice that Figure 3.4 also suggests when the group should have the discussions. In this way, the instructor is also assisting the group with time management.

4. Identify specific web tools for the group to use. There are so many tools that students can use to interact and collaborate online. The overwhelming number of choices can make decision-making time consuming. This can be problematic for working adults with families who have only the weekends to get assignments completed. Selecting a specific tool can facilitate group collaboration.

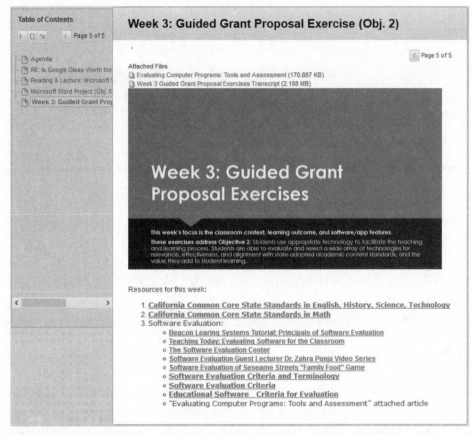

Figure 3.3 First of four parts of a major project scaffolded throughout an eight-week course

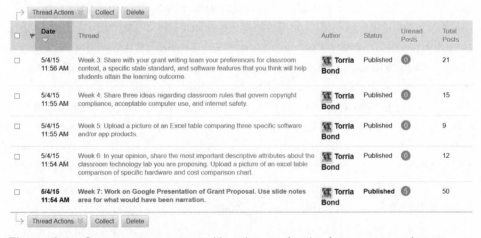

Figure 3.4 Group space prepared in advance for the four conversations needed to complete the group project

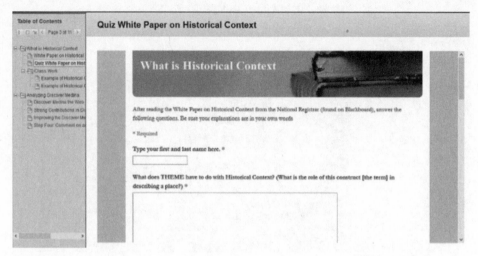

Figure 3.5 Google form embedded on a content page to collect student responses to a quiz
Source: Image courtesy of Shannon Conley Kurjian from Medina County

Google Docs is a web-based productivity suite that contains applications for word processing, spreadsheets, presentations, and forms. These are convenient applications for designing presentations or fill-in and short answer forms that can be embedded into the course page. Because the documents update in real time, they can also be used to facilitate brainstorming and small group collaboration in an online class. Shannon Conley Kurjian is a high school social studies teacher in Medina County, Ohio, who used Google forms to capture students' responses to a reading assignment, as seen in Figure 3.5. Similarly, a Google presentation was embedded in the small group discussion space for a collaborative project, as shown in Figure 3.6. As of this writing, you can link to the documents you create using Google Docs, but Google Docs doesn't offer embed codes (yet). The iframe is an HTML code that *may* allow a web page to be embedded in an LMS or website when an embed code is not available.

The Google form and presentation embedded into content pages in Figures 3.5 and 3.6 used this iframe code:

```
<iframe width="100%" height="400" src="https://www.PLACE THE
TEXT OF THE URL HERE></iframe>
```

Figure 3.6 Google presentation embedded in the small group discussion space for synchronous or asynchronous collaboration

Rather than thinking of an iframe as complicated HTML coding, think of it as a family recipe handed down from generation to generation. It contains "ingredients" for the width, height, and source of the media to be embedded. The iframe can be one of your best friends, helping you to embed content into a course where an embed code is not provided. The iframe shown here can be used just like your favorite recipe by placing the URL of the page you want to embed between the quotation marks following `src=`.

HOW DO I PROVIDE INSTRUCTION ONLINE?

Once you have determined learning outcomes, objectives, and assessment measures and gathered instructional procedures, information, and resources, you can simplify constructing a lesson by using or modifying existing educational models of instruction. There are many educational instructional models (Estes, Mintz, & Gunter, 2011). Some, for example, are useful for helping students perceive cause and effect, making generalizations from data, analyzing text, learning new concepts, or problem solving. Given an educational model of instruction appropriate for your learning outcomes and objectives, consider identifying consistent content elements that you can apply throughout the construction of the course. Types of content elements might include a lesson overview, list of objectives, anticipatory activities, lesson presentation, current event, discussion or debate forum, assignments, resources, case study, journal reflections, blog posts, experiential exercises, observations, and self-assessments, just to name a few. It would not be practical to have all of these content elements in every week of a course. However, consistently using a few of them contributes to the perception of an organized and easy-to-navigate course.

To illustrate this idea, let's build a lesson based on the educational instructional model referred to as "direct instruction," a common instructional model useful for teaching specific skills, facts, and foundational principles of a discipline (Estes, Mintz, & Gunter, 2011). The steps to implement this model vary, but generally include the following:

1. An activity to gain attention and provide a context to the skill, fact, or foundational principal being presented

2. An instructional presentation that includes how to perform a skill, the relevance of a particular fact, or the application of a foundational principal

3. Supervised practice based on an exemplar or demonstration of the assignment expectation, in which the instructor provides detailed feedback

4. An activity that provides the learner with unsupervised practice to determine if the objective was attained or needs to be retaught

While this educational instructional model has roots in the implementation of a lesson in face-to-face classrooms, let's consider one way the sequence of steps can be modified for fully online delivery. In addition, we'll apply the L.I.T.E. skills to the visual design of a lesson in an LMS or website.

THE MARSHMALLOW CHALLENGE LESSON AND THE DIRECT INSTRUCTION MODEL FOR TEACHING SKILLS, FACTS, OR FOUNDATIONAL PRINCIPLES

The lesson being shared is the first of five units in a graduate course on trends in science education, contributed by Jennifer Perkins, an instructional designer from Eastern Kentucky University. The lesson was written in collaboration with a subject matter expert and constructed in Blackboard by the designer. The screenshots of the lesson have been modified to offer suggestions for applying the L.I.T.E. skills and an educational instructional model for lesson presentation in the online format.

This lesson introduces teacher education students to the concept of engineering for elementary and middle schools students. By the end of this introductory lesson, students will be able to

- Compare and contrast the human endeavors of science and engineering

- Explain the concept of technology in the context of engineering and society

- Identify technology in terms of object, system, or process (iterative process)

The direct instruction model is useful for teaching skills, facts, and foundational principles. In this lesson, the skill students learn is the iterative process. Specifically, they learn to generate multiple prototypes on their way to a final result. Facts include distinguishing between the concepts of science and engineering. Knowledge includes differentiating between the engineering and science perspectives of technology. Throughout this lesson, notice how the pedagogical practices are enhanced through the L.I.T.E. skills. Also notice that design elements are contributed by both the student and the instructor.

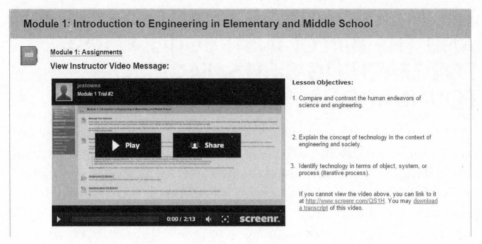

Figure 3.7 Module entry point contains video message from instructor and lesson objectives

State Objectives for the Lesson

Prior to entering the module, lesson objectives are clearly stated. As educators we know that objectives connected to what students already know increases retention and keeps students focused on the learning outcome. An overview of the lesson—its objectives, lesson activities, and navigational elements in Blackboard—is provided through an instructor-created video, shown in Figure 3.7. Each assignment in the module is briefly explained.

L.I.T.E. Visual Design Points: A table is used to align an embedded video message from the instructor next to a numbered list of objectives. A link to download the transcript is provided for students who need or prefer text. A direct link to the embedded video is also provided just in case the embedded video is not visible after the content page loads. While some design approaches may choose to upload the video separately from the learning objectives and file links, the integration of all three elements into one content item contributes to a low folder depth ratio and a symmetrically balanced visual appearance.

How to: Locate the table function on the text editor of the LMS or website being used. Create three columns and five rows. Merge the cells in the left column and type the word EMBED in caps as shown in Figure 3.8.

This will be a helpful aid when you look at the HTML code view and need to insert the embed code in the proper location among the other code elements. When you access the HTML code view, this will prompt you to paste the video embed code in the correct location, as shown in Figure 3.9.

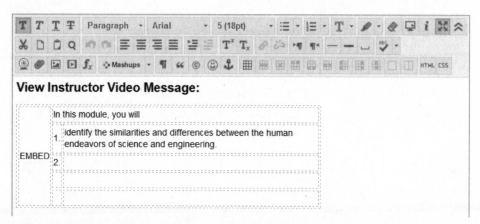

Figure 3.8   A table used to manage alignment of text and video

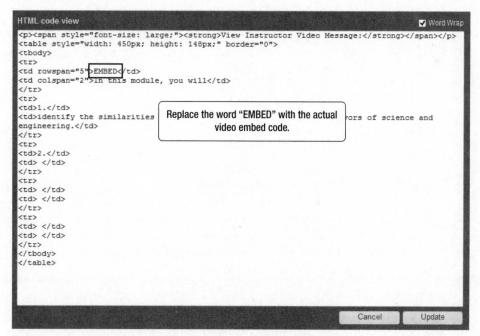

Figure 3.9   The word EMBED will be replaced with code in the HTML code view

Merge the first row of cells in the middle and right columns. This is where explanatory text will be placed. The middle column is just for the item numbers. The right column will contain the text for each numbered item. This can be seen in Figure 3.8.

Review Previously Learned Material or Identify Prior Knowledge

This step in the model explores preconceived notions students already have about the concepts of science and engineering. The tool shown in Figure 3.10, a variant on a Venn diagram, is used to help students compare

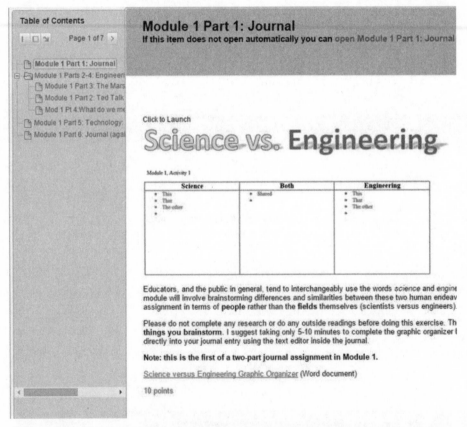

Figure 3.10 A comparison tool used to see what students know about the concepts of science and engineering prior to instruction

and contrast the two concepts. It can serve as a diagnostic assessment for the online instructor and can guide additional comments made to students via discussion forums or instructor announcements.

L.I.T.E. Visual Design Points: In the figure, "Science vs. Engineering" is presented using WordArt (decorative text), a typographical strategy used to focus student attention on the objective of comparing and contrasting the two concepts. The tool being used is displayed as an embedded graphic in which the instructor has modeled the expected writing style. Text is brief and surrounded by white space to enhance readability and legibility. Links to the assignment document, as well as the assignment directions, are provided in the assignment submission area for ease of navigation and clarity of instruction. Because an image of the WordArt was taken, the alt tag field is used to describe the words in the image to enhance accessibility to individuals using a screen reader or other assistive devices.

How To: In this case, the WordArt feature from PowerPoint 2013 was used to create the "Science vs. Engineering" image. Then a free screen capture tool, Jing by TechSmith, was used to capture the image. The image was placed on a PowerPoint slide with the Venn diagram; then the full PowerPoint slide was captured and saved as an image. This was the image uploaded to Blackboard with the alt tag phrase "Science vs. Engineering and Comparison Diagram Contrasting the Two Concepts (Figure 3.11)."

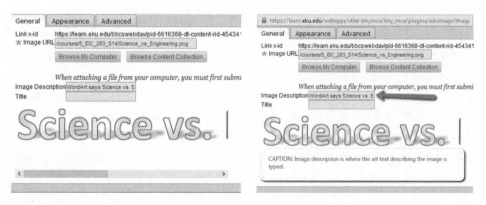

Figure 3.11 The image description field is where alt tag text is placed for screen readers to verbally describe an image

Step 1: Gain the attention of the learner and provide a context for the skill, fact, or foundational principal being presented.

When someone says they were "hooked" from the moment a movie began or from the very beginning of a book, they're referring to the anticipation they had for what would happen next. The instructor for this lesson presents an experiential exercise to heighten the students' anticipation for the upcoming lesson and its activities. The experiential exercise that learners do offline is referred to as the Marshmallow Challenge. The exercise is meant to introduce them to the basic process of engineering, using a hands-on design challenge as shown in Figure 3.12. After students complete the activity offline, they post pictures of their engagement in the experience in the designated blog space as shown in Figure 3.13 and respond to the instructor's questions regarding their experience. The instructor can see students engaged in the design challenge and make connections to their experience as the lesson progresses through discussion forums or perhaps instructor video messages. The instructor creates a common experience for everyone in the course as a foundation for a discussion about engineering. The hands-on activity serves as an anticipatory set or attention getter for the material presented in the remainder of the lesson as well as the course. The instructor can draw on students' experience with this activity as the lesson progresses.

L.I.T.E. Visual Design Points: A self-paced, illustrated slide presentation of the activity directions, shown in Figure 3.12, is embedded on the content page surrounded by minimal text and plenty of white space. Students maintain their location in Blackboard while reviewing the directions. The blog space needs few words to describe the assignment because the visuals let students know that they are going to be discussing their success or failures, as seen in Figure 3.13. In that way the image is more than decoration on the content page but also provides assignment information. Students post images of their engagement in the design challenge, contributing to a visually engaging blog space for their peers.

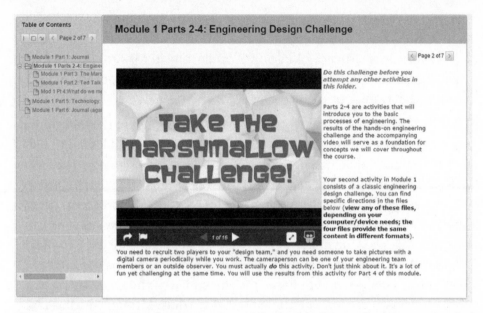

Figure 3.12 PowerPoint presentation of design challenge directions uploaded to SlideShare and embedded in the content page

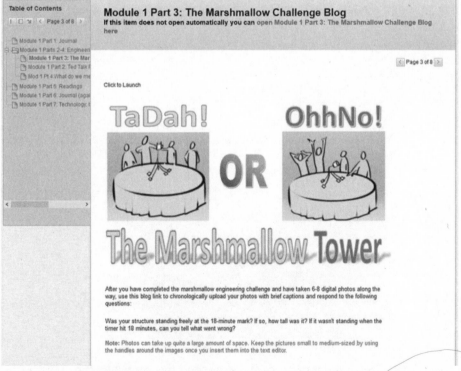

Figure 3.13 Blog space where students post evidence of design challenge completion and respond to instructor questions about the experience

Step 2: Present instructional information that includes how to perform a skill, the relevance of a particular fact, or the application of a foundational principal.

At this stage in the model, the instructor continues to present the background knowledge needed to grasp upcoming concepts. New information is layered on top of reviewed material. In this lesson, four new pieces of information are layered on top of the design challenge. First, a TED Talk video is presented to discuss the significance of the design challenge. Second, the iterative process, a foundational concept for the course, is presented. Third, a broad view of technology is presented, and last, assigned readings are made available.

L.I.T.E. Visual Design Points: Rather than embedding the required video into a separate content item, it is embedded in the same area in which students access the questions in PDF or .docx format, which is also the assignment submission area. As Figure 3.14 shows, adding these items

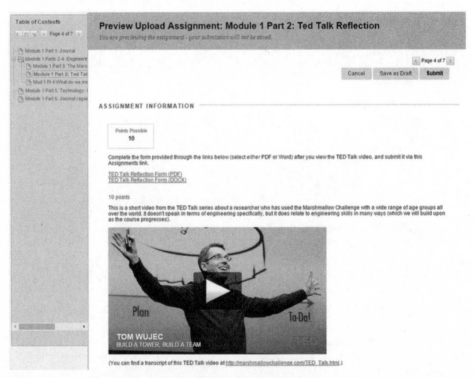

Figure 3.14   The amount of content is managed by combining the video and forms in the assignment submission space

to the same assignment area prevents cognitive overload by keeping the list of items in the table of contents to a minimum.

Step 3: Supervise practice based on an exemplar or demonstration of the assignment expectation in which the instructor provides detailed feedback.

In face-to-face classes, supervised practice is the portion of the lesson when the instructor models the expectation and observes students as they attempt to fulfill that expectation. In an asynchronous course, the line between presenting new information and modeling expectations is not linear. As new information is presented, the instructor informally checks for understanding simultaneously. In this case, the instructor provides a blog space allowing students to reflect on the video. In addition, the instructor gives students the opportunity to self-assess and ensure they are moving toward the lesson objectives. The simultaneous experience of providing content information and allowing students to reflect on the presentation allows the instructor to respond to students individually and collectively for feedback. Figure 3.15 shows the instructor providing a blog space to confirm that students recognize the iterative process as experienced in the design challenge and presented in the TED Talk and other instructional materials.

L.I.T.E. Visual Design Points: WordArt focuses student attention to the topic to be addressed. An illustration of the iterative process is shown on the blog page with a brief text description of the term and the question students are to address as seen in Figure 3.15. Again, both the image and the text are surrounded by the white space needed for legibility and readability.

Step 4: Provide the learner with an unsupervised activity to determine whether the objective was attained or needs to be retaught.

All objectives, except one, have been assessed through the review of responses to questions posed in the various blog spaces set up by the instructor. After the new material is presented and opportunities for supervised practice provided, the instructor is ready to ascertain whether or not the lesson outcomes have been achieved. In this case, the only objective

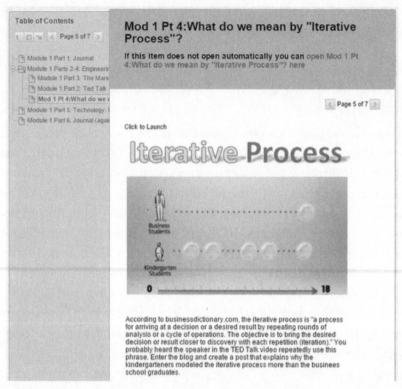

Mod 1 Pt 4:What do we mean by "Iterative Process"?

If this item does not open automatically you can open Mod 1 Pt 4:What do we mean by "Iterative Process"? here

Page 5 of 7

Click to Launch

Iterative Process

Business Students

Kindergarten Students

0   18

According to businessdictionary.com, the iterative process is "a process for arriving at a decision or a desired result by repeating rounds of analysis or a cycle of operations. The objective is to bring the desired decision or result closer to discovery with each repetition (iteration)." You probably heard the speaker in the TED Talk video repeatedly use this phrase. Enter the blog and create a post that explains why the kindergarteners modeled the iterative process more than the businees school graduates.

Figure 3.15   Blog space created to confirm student understanding and provide feedback

that hasn't been assessed is comparing and contrasting science and engineering. The instructor chooses to administer the same Venn diagram used to build on what students knew at the beginning to see how their understanding has changed at the conclusion of the activities as shown in Figure 3.10. Since this is the end of the introductory lesson, students and the instructor can compare viewpoints before and after instruction as both an assessment and a meaningful learning exercise.

How Much Content Is Too Much Content?

"A teacher's value is not in the information stored in their head, but rather their ability to pull together the best learning resources to produce a desired outcome (Orlando, 2010)." Given the vast amount of content available on any given subject, an instructor's/trainer's worth lies in the ability to vet the information and arrange it in a developmentally appropriate manner for learners. If this sounds like content curation, you're right. Content curators and instructors/trainers have several things in common. They both vet a lot of information to save readers or learners time in acquiring what they need to know. They also bring to the forefront the information perceived as most valuable and helpful in reaching a given aim. While curators may stop at this point, instructors/trainers take it a step further and sequence information to help learners achieve a specific outcome within a given time frame. The challenge for the instructors/trainer is making sure learners don't feel like they are drinking water from a fire hose as they acquire new information!

Strategies to Avoid Content Overload

Have you ever looked at the progress bar of a required online compliance training and noticed that you're on slide 10 of 210 slides? Or taken an online class and in week one had a list of 25 content items? How did you feel? Overwhelmed doesn't begin to describe the self-doubt learners may feel as they question whether they can really complete the task laid out before them. They start to wonder how they will get it all done in the midst of working full time, taking care of family, and balancing a host of conflicting priorities. You can help to minimize these feelings by managing the folder depth ratio in an online course.

For purposes of our discussion, folder depth ratio refers to the combination of instructional materials and folders located in the same modular space. It includes the number of content items and the organization structure of content folders. Folder depth ratio affects the number of mouse clicks it takes a learner to access a particular piece of content. A high folder depth ratio occurs when a list of instructional content items are placed in a folder and the folder is placed in a folder repeatedly, as shown in Figure 1.1 of Chapter One. While it seems like a good idea to place like items in separate folders, the end result leaves students guessing where a particular piece of content can be found. Let's say you are looking for BBQ sauce in the grocery store. Will I find the BBQ sauce in the meat department by the ribs or the chicken? Or will I find the BBQ sauce on the condiments aisle with the ketchup and mustard? If I have a recipe for BBQ chicken salad, is it possible the BBQ sauce is located next to the lettuce in the produce aisle? Folders within folders make up a complex organizational structure that can be difficult to navigate.

In contrast, a low folder depth ratio provides a simple organizational structure. Having a limited number of content items in one folder per unit of study is ideal. This keeps the design L.I.T.E. If a hierarchical structure is needed, keep the number of folders to the bare minimum. Creating small instructional modules helps students navigate to a given resource within two to three mouse clicks.

Let's look at an instructional module with out-of-control content to see how we can repurpose our old acronym M.E.S.S.—which highlighted four problematic elements of an online course that can make it, well, a *mess*— to help manage the amount of content presented in an online course. As a reminder, those problematic elements were Many new technologies, Excessive amounts of content, Several related content items, Supplemental resources mixed with required resources. A reworking of M.E.S.S. reminds us to

- Minimize new technology introduced to students
- Eliminate nice-to-know (but not need-to-know) content
- Streamline related content
- Separate supplemental from required resources

CASE STUDY: THE INSTRUCTIONAL DESIGN OF AN INTRODUCTION TO SOCIOLOGY COURSE

In one of my first course design efforts in collaboration with a subject matter expert, my initial efforts exhibited some very common errors. I created *lots* of content items, required students to use several technologies, mingled important content requiring no action on the student's part with content that required student responses, and wove too many support materials in with required materials. The result was a difficult-to-navigate course that lacked clarity and required students to spend more time on learning new technologies than learning the course content. To illustrate the challenges of the first iteration of the course, let's take a look at the first week of instruction.

As with most courses, the first day or week is filled with community-building activities such as icebreakers and low-risk academic and social discussion, intermingled with foundational instruction needed to understand more advanced concepts. In the first iteration of the course, the week one instructional module had over sixteen content items:

- An overview of the week's learning objectives, with a list of items to review or complete
- A course welcome video that included a review of the course syllabus
- A list of objectives for the reading assignment
- A comprehension quiz on the chapter readings
- A video on the sociological imagination
- A video on Christian sociology
- A trailer from the movie *Forrest Gump*
- A tutorial on how to use a piece of required technology in the course
- An introductory discussion forum with a discussion question on the sociological imagination evident in *Forrest Gump*
- An explanation of the culminating assignment—a service learning project requiring the use of a wiki
- A content item requesting that students visit a religious service in preparation for week two's learning objectives
- An invitation to the instructor's office hours
- A video on navigating the course in the learning management system
- An item about software applications that may be needed
- An item explaining what to do if you need special accommodations
- An explanation of the small group sociologist activity
- A tutorial on using the text editor

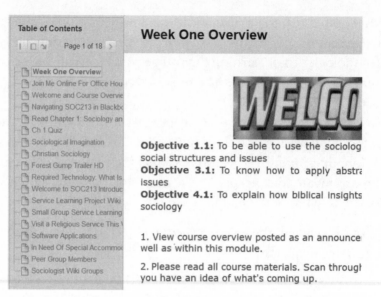

Week One Overview

Objective 1.1: To be able to use the sociolog social structures and issues
Objective 3.1: To know how to apply abstr issues
Objective 4.1: To explain how biblical insights sociology

1. View course overview posted as an announce well as within this module.

2. Please read all course materials. Scan throug you have an idea of what's coming up.

Figure 3.16 Excessive content in week one can be visually overwhelming

Figure 3.16 depicts these items in the LMS. What a M.E.S.S.! Why do I say that? First, there are a number of new technologies that students taking a two hundred–level course and new to online learning may not have encountered. Therefore, content items that explain the technologies must be included. Second, there are several content items that are important but don't directly relate to the objectives of the instructional unit. Third, there are several related content items that could be streamlined to reduce the folder depth ratio. Last, instructional materials that require student action are mixed in with those that require no action on the student's part. These items can and should be separated.

Most entry-level courses will have students new to the institution and new to the online environment. A list of tasks like this one would probably make students feel like they had to be technology experts to complete assignments online, have discussions online, work in groups online, and navigate the learning management systems, particularly in an entry-level course primarily with first- and second-year college students. Even if the learning objectives are clearly stated, tutorials for navigating the course and using LMS features are present, and a variety of multimedia is used for good instruction, the high folder depth ratio of required content mixed with supportive resources, plus the new technologies, pulls the learner's focus away from the learning objectives.

Minimize the Use of New Technologies

Since we want the use of technology to enhance our online course rather than become a learning objective on its own, let's look at the number of technologies integrated into the course that can contribute to content overload. In just week one, students learn they need to be able to use Voice-Thread, blogs, groups, and wikis throughout an eight week course. As a result, this week one module contains a VoiceThread tutorial, a text editor tutorial showing how to upload various multimedia items into a wiki, and an item explaining how to join a group. However, students are not shown how to use the blog feature or access small group tools. One could argue that the required use of unfamiliar technologies contributes to learner frustration and increases the folder depth ratio. But by requiring the use of one type of new technology, I eliminated the need for additional content items to explain the technology. In this case, the group assignment and the wiki assignments were removed and revised to make continued use of the assignment tool. By removing the added technologies, we've reduced the folder depth ratio by two content items.

Eliminate Nice-to-Know Content Items

This is really hard to do. We want students to have all the resources we can make available to them for independent exploration and personal growth. However, the instructional module may not be the best place for all types of resources. Many syllabi have a section for recommended or suggested resources. Because we make resources available to students, they don't feel overwhelmed. In fact, many students appreciate knowing what's available. However, when those resources are mixed in with required resources and activities and students can't tell the difference, frustration sets in.

As we continue to examine the remaining items in the week one folder, we find several nice-to-have but not essential items. For example, the content item for visiting a religious service is related to another instructional module, as is the information on the small group sociologist assignment. While it's nice to give students a heads-up into upcoming weeks, this content item is best suited for the week in which the related learning objectives are addressed. Given that the assignments are part of the syllabus, discussed in the video overview for the course, a sentence or two embedded in the weekly overview under the title "in preparation for next week" may be enough to encourage students to plan ahead. By removing these items from the week one folder, we've reduced the folder depth ratio by another two items.

Streamline Related Content Items

Several items in the week one folder shown in Figure 3.16 are related to one another. Let's see which items we can combine to reduce the number of items in the table of contents. A good example of combining related items is illustrated in Figure 3.17. Instead of having separate items for the

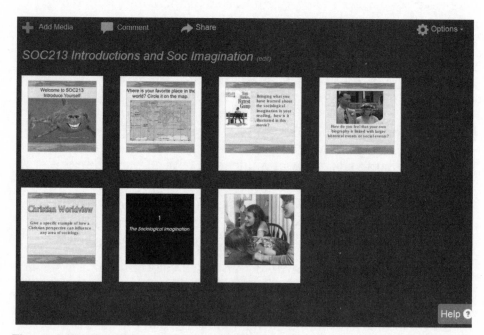

Figure 3.17 Two short videos required for the assignment were merged into the VoiceThread player, reducing the number of content items

course introduction, a discussion of the sociological imagination in the movie *Forrest Gump*, and an area to upload documents related to the task, all three are combined into the same content item. However, there are still more items in the week one folder that can be combined with this one to reduce the number of items in the folder. For example, the *Forrest Gump* trailer is actually related to the course introduction and discussion of the movie. Therefore we can add the trailer to the description of the assignment. In addition, the videos explaining the sociological imagination and Christian sociology are both foundational concepts in the course and required discussion items following student introductions. We can further reduce the folder depth ratio by uploading those items to the VoiceThread player in the assignment as shown in Figure 3.17.

Lastly, look for a content item that contains reading objectives and a reading comprehension quiz in the top left of Figure 3.18. The content item contains just an image with text. The top right content item of Figure 3.18 contains only the link to access the reading comprehension quiz. There is plenty of space to add the image and the text from the top left image to the top right image, resulting in the bottom image containing all three. Combining related content items is one strategy for reducing the folder depth ratio. By combining content directions with the assignment submission areas, we have reduced the folder depth ratio by three more content items.

Separate Important but Unrelated Content Items

Taking another look at our original list of content items, there are a couple of items that are very important to student success in the course but are not related to the week's assignment activities. For example, it's important for students to access the video welcome in which the instructor is introduced, the syllabus is reviewed, and a general course overview is provided. However, it is not essential to the week one instructional content. How can we make those items available to students without overloading the instructional module with too many content items? One possibility is to create a separate folder or module for those items. I've personally gravitated toward

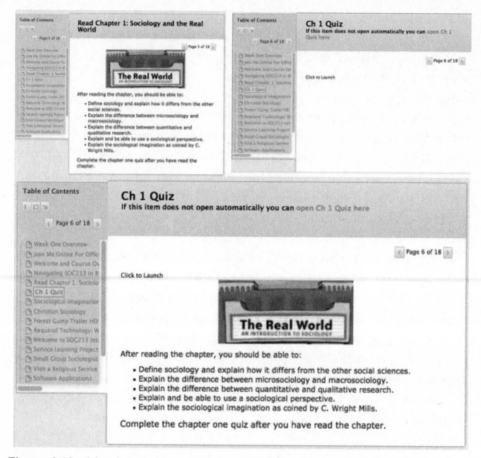

Figure 3.18 Merging reading objectives into the quiz space helps prevent content overload

the concept of the "week zero" module shared with me during a forum discussion for one of the online workshops I attended. The week zero folder would contain all the information students need to be successful in the course, such as an introductory video on navigating the course in the learning management system, tutorials for the use of required technologies, software applications needed, online office hour technologies, and other institutional polices such as requesting special accommodations. You could also link those items to the course navigation menu. Some institutions place a link entitled "syllabus" directly on the course navigation menu. The video could also be moved from the week one instructional

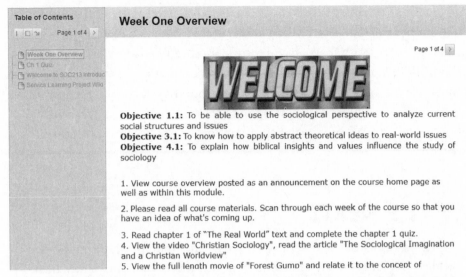

Week One Overview

Objective 1.1: To be able to use the sociological perspective to analyze current social structures and issues
Objective 3.1: To know how to apply abstract theoretical ideas to real-world issues
Objective 4.1: To explain how biblical insights and values influence the study of sociology

1. View course overview posted as an announcement on the course home page as well as within this module.

2. Please read all course materials. Scan through each week of the course so that you have an idea of what's coming up.

3. Read chapter 1 of "The Real World" text and complete the chapter 1 quiz.
4. View the video "Christian Sociology", read the article "The Sociological Imagination and a Christian Worldview"
5. View the full length movie of "Forest Gump" and relate it to the concept of

Figure 3.19 Content was reduced from more than sixteen items to four by minimizing use of new technologies, eliminating nice-to-know content, streamlining related content, and separating supplemental from required resources

module and embedded in a folder that contains the syllabus. Content descriptions and multimedia on the folder is a good visual and a good use of space to reduce the folder depth ratio. Moving these important but unrelated content items from the week one instructional module reduces the folder depth ratio by another five content items.

By combining related content items, minimizing new technology introduced to students, moving important but unrelated content items to new location, and eliminating nice-to-know content, we have arrived at a week one learning module containing just four content items. We have removed twelve content items from the instructional module. For students, the content shown in Figure 3.19 is far less overwhelming than the same content in Figure 3.16.

SUMMARY

Engaging learners through asynchronous discussions and group projects is one of the greatest challenges instructors face. Suggestions for constructing the online discussion forum and developing collaborative assignments through scaffolding were offered. The use of educational models of instruction can provide the structure needed to present lessons online. To illustrate this idea, the direct instruction model was presented. We also discussed ways to reduce content overload by minimizing required technologies, eliminating nice-to-know content, streamlining related content, and separating supplemental resources from required resources.

WHAT'S NEXT?

Today, those of us in the teaching and learning field are standing on the shoulders of giants. Many educators and trainers have gone before us to share dynamic strategies, techniques, and tools from which to teach in any delivery format. There is no need to start from scratch when it comes to teaching and learning. Continue to build upon the work of others by considering the following activities:

1. Given the discussion board features available in your course building environment, determine how you will foster the common courtesies of face-to-face communication online.

2. Locate an instructional model that you can use for a lesson in your course. Identify the modifications needed to adapt the model for asynchronous online delivery. What consistent content elements will you use throughout the lesson or course?

3. Use the L.I.T.E. skills as a framework for constructing a lesson in an LMS or website.

4. Create an introductory week of an online course, giving consideration to the strategies presented here to avoid content overload. Explain your design choices to a colleague. Solicit their feedback on the number of items in the introductory week and whether or not content can be eliminated, moved to another location, or combined with other items. Do your technology choices enhance the presentation of the content and the activities to be completed?

4

HOW DO I INTEGRATE MULTIMEDIA?

*While the information you are providing to your learners should be of high quality,
you should also have in mind that the method of presentation is just as essential.*
—Christopher Pappas, founder of The e-learning Industry's Network

Motion picture making is easily a multibillion dollar industry. Seemingly, no expense is spared for good photography, costumes, actors, on-location shoots in international lands, directing, filming, and editing. After all the time and financial investment in creating a movie, can you imagine what would happen to that investment if marketing and promotions consisted of a sticky note that read "Come see this movie"?

As an online instructor or trainer, you spend considerable time identifying measurable learning outcomes, creating authentic assessments, designing relevant learning activities, gathering resources, sequencing instruction, ensuring curricular alignment, orienting students to the online environment, troubleshooting technical issues—the list goes on. After all the meticulous time and care given to the development of the course, is it possible to display the course content in a way that fosters interest and curiosity about the content? Just as a three-minute movie trailer creates interest in a full-length feature film, how you present your instructional materials in your online course or training can inspire interest and encourage persistence through course completion. To that end, let's consider ways in which multimedia content—that is, any combination of text, audio, video, images, graphics, hypermedia, simulations, and various interactive learning objects—can be integrated into an online course or training.

READABILITY AND LEGIBILITY

According to Allen and Seyman's (2014) report "Grade Change: Tracking Online Education in the United States," 33.5 percent of higher education students now take at least one online course. The number of students taking at least one online course has increased by more than 6 percent from the previous year. Students taking online courses spend a significant amount of time looking at computer screens on their desktops and mobile devices. The Pew Research Foundation published an increase in e-book reading from 2011 to 2014 (Desilver, 2014). In 2011, of all the adults over eighteen who read a book that year, 17 percent read an e-book. In 2014 the number increased by 28 percent, with more reading on tablets and cell phones than on desktops and laptops (Greenfield, 2014). This being the case, issues of legibility and readability are paramount. What's the difference? When you think of sloppy penmanship, your first thought is usually *I can't read this.* I can't even make out the letters. In contrast, when we say text is hard to read, it's implied that the text can be read, but it requires considerable effort. For example, the text in the image in Figure 4.1 is legible because we can read the individual letters. However, the text

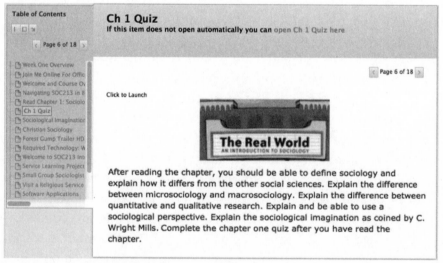

Figure 4.1 The text in this image is legible

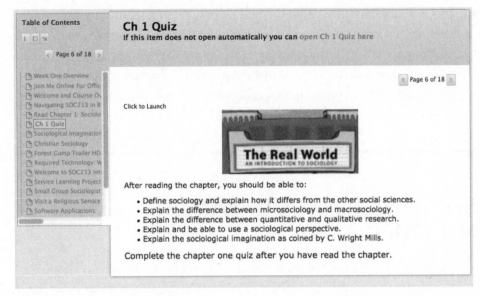

Figure 4.2   White space contributes positively to readability

in Figure 4.2 is more readable because the additional white space created by the bullet list format makes comprehending the message easier, even though the text is the same in both figures.

Delivering a course or training online requires that careful consideration is given to both legibility and readability. Legibility is most affected by font style and size. Decorative fonts look great as a headline in 48 point on attention-getting flyers. However, the same decorative font in 12 point can become illegible for large amounts of text. For educational and training purposes, nondecorative serif or sans-serif fonts work best—that is, Arial, Verdana, Times New Roman, and so on. Typically 10, 12, or 14 point fonts are common for most educational reading purposes. Any smaller than 10 point type, the lowercase letters of c, e, and o become difficult to distinguish. Going larger than 14 point type can negatively impact readability. It's a good idea to limit the number of font types and sizes used throughout the course or training. Different font types and sizes used in close proximity can negatively affect both readability and legibility.

It's important that you not feel you are wasting space by not covering an entire page with text or graphics. Readability is most enhanced by white space, which allows specific text or images to become the focal point of the page. Typographic elements such as bullets and numbers help create white space that allows your eyes to scan the page and comprehend the written message with ease. Contrast between text and background colors also helps the eyes scan the page and comprehend written messages. This contrast can be created through color, thick lines of bold text, thin slanted lines of italics, and underlined text. Most text editors allow you to manipulate all of these to create white space.

STRATEGIES FOR DISPLAYING MULTIMEDIA

Let's start with a simple strategy: the use of tables. Tables are available in most "what you see is what you get" (WYSIWYG) editors. Tables are not just for organizing or arranging information. Dr. Larysa Nadolyny, an assistant professor at Iowa State University, used a table to display text and video on the same content page. Tables can be used to display a video in one cell and text in another cell for a side by side display without using code. Cells can be merged as needed to create a balanced appearance in the table on the content page. With tables, you can put a bullet in a cell alone and the next cell can contain the bulleted information. This keeps bullets, numberings, and text all in alignment with any multimedia being displayed. Figure 4.3 shows a content page with text in the first left column, and embedded video and text in the next column. Figure 4.4 shows the text editor view of the content page, displaying the text and the videos with table cells. In the HTML view, the embed code is placed in between the code for a table cell. Because I know just enough code to be dangerous, I type the word EMBED in capital letters into a cell while in the text editor view. Then I look for the word EMBED while in the HTML code view and replace the word with the actual embed code. (This was shown in Figures 3.7 and 3.8 in Chapter Three.) For additional HTML learning resources, visit W3Schools.Com for a free HTML tutorial or do a Google search on "learn html free."

Figure 4.3 Use the table feature to format multimedia

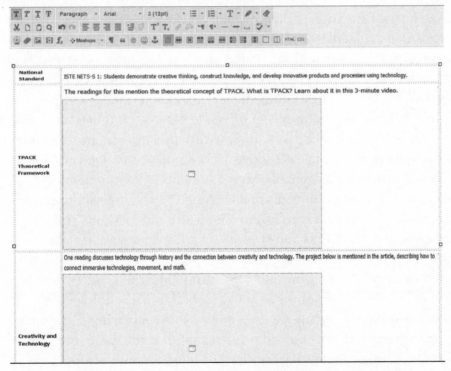

Figure 4.4 Text editor view of the content page shown in Figure 4.3

USING MULTIMEDIA FOR INSTRUCTION

As I'm writing this book, my son is a first-semester college freshman taking an anatomy physiology course. The course presents a tremendous number of new concepts that students must understand in a short period of time. The instructional resources available included the textbook, publisher-prepared PowerPoint slides with bullet points, and face-to-face class lectures supported with PowerPoint slides and diagrams. The textbook and PowerPoint presentations provided instructional information using one medium—text, and lots of it. I can still remember the times I fell asleep reading a textbook (and not because I was sleepy). The instructor's one-hour lecture supported by PowerPoint slides with bullet points and diagrams engaged the auditory and visual senses. But for many learners, an hour of listening to new information, especially when delivered in a soothing monotone voice, can cause their minds to wander, dull the senses, and put them to sleep (please tell me I'm not the only one). In *Teaching with the Brain in Mind,* author Eric Jensen discusses the challenges of extended periods of focused attention without mental breaks and active engagement. It is suggested that adult learners can focus for fifteen to eighteen minutes of direct instruction; this will vary based on a learner's prior experience with the content and other social and emotional factors (Jenson, 2005). This is a situation in which using multimedia for instruction can be of value.

Instructional presentations of fifteen to eighteen minutes are focused on specific learning objectives. To fit within this time frame, information needs to focus on a single objective, be "chunked" into logical segments of material you can reasonably expect students to comprehend and retain. One way to ensure reasonable chunking and logical progression of content is to apply research-based instructional methods and learning strategies. Both methods and strategies are implemented in steps, and those steps can be used as sections within a lesson. One such research-based strategy is comparing and contrasting (Marzano, 2001), which is used in a variety of inquiry-based instructional methodologies to foster critical thinking. A technique used to facilitate comparing and contrasting is the application of metaphor. A metaphor is the use of one object or concept (often something familiar) to illustrate another (perhaps unfamiliar); for example, an ocean to illustrate the depth of one's feelings. An instructor could model this technique in the content area when students need to recall vast amounts of conceptual vocabulary and could suggest that students use the technique as a study strategy.

Let's apply the technique of metaphor to facilitate recall of the function, location, and activation of muscle tissue discussed in an anatomy and physiology course. Our purpose is to help connect new concepts to something that is already familiar. In my son's case, he had been playing basketball since he was in elementary school. He played on his middle school and high school teams as well as intensely competitive travel basketball teams with athletes pursuing college scholarships. Given what he knew about basketball, I encouraged him to apply the following steps to help him remember the structure of muscle tissues and, in his own study time, to apply the steps to help him remember the location, function, and activation of muscle tissues.

1. *Choose a topic in which you are well versed.* This can be any topic under the sun. As an instructor modeling this strategy for students, select a topic you enjoy. Even if students don't identify with your topic, they can be encouraged to use their own. For this example, let's use the concept of "setting a screen" in basketball and brainstorm everything we know about that topic. First, my son and I know that the purpose of setting a screen is to make space between offensive and defensive players to create an opportunity for the offensive player to shoot the basketball. Second, we know that a legal screen occurs when another offensive player plants his body vertically between the shooter and defensive player without leaning forward or backward. Third, we know there are different ways to set a screen—that is, down screen, ball screen, back screen, away screen (Basketball Breakthrough, 2015). We could brainstorm more on this topic, but for now let's work with these three points.

2. *Identify the concepts to be learned.* In this case, the content provided by the instructor included the purpose of muscle tissue; three types of muscle tissue; and the structure, location, function, and activation of each of those muscle tissues.

3. *Connect the new material to the known topic.* The goal is to find ways in which the new material is similar to the known topic. In this case, we're going to list the ways in which setting a screen in basketball is similar to the structure of muscle tissues.

   a. *Both involve movement.* Screens facilitate player movement that leads to shooting or passing the basketball. Muscles facilitate bodily movement, whether voluntary or involuntary.

   b. *Parallel positioning.* The screen is positioned parallel to the defender, just as muscle tissue fibers are positioned parallel to one another.

   c. *Both act as barriers.* The screen acts as a barrier between the offensive and defensive player; muscle tissue acts as a barrier between the skeletal frame and the skin.

As an instructor, I can screencast an explanation of the technique and build an interactive file with rollover text to visually display the similarities and differences, as shown in Figure 4.5. As a study technique, I could provide students with Venn diagrams and encourage students to use this technique for concepts that are hard for them to recall using other techniques, as shown in Figure 4.6.

The challenge comes with finding a place to store multimedia files, which are often large and somewhat taxing for students to access through direct uploads to learning management systems (LMSs) or online storage locations using the internet connections available to them. Just as we recommend that videos be hosted on a site that allows sharing, maintaining your own instructor website will allow you to directly share interactive multimedia presentations from it. As an instructor, I prefer to manage my own content, so I can update it and share it as the need arises. Maintaining your own website is becoming easier as technologies improve.

The authoring tool that produced the content in Figure 4.5 had the option to output the file as a SCORM file. SCORM stands for "sharable content object reference model"; it is a standard protocol that allows

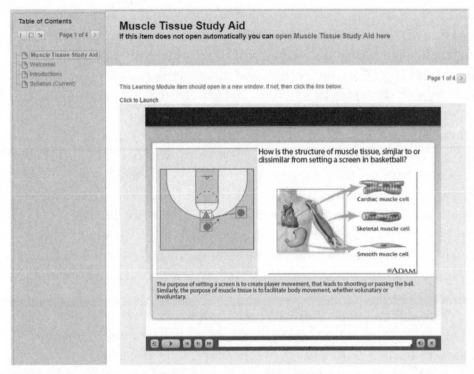

Figure 4.5 Adobe Captivate file output as SCORM file and uploaded to Blackboard with reporting features connected to grade center

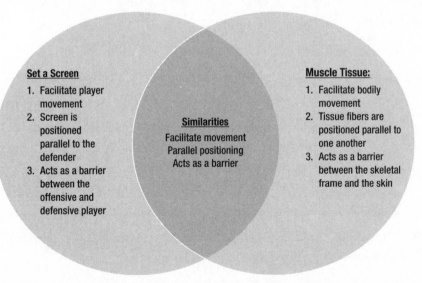

Figure 4.6 Venn diagram used to apply the metaphor technique to recall information

interactive elements in an e-learning course to communicate with the assessment features in an LMS. SCORM files are another great way to engage learners with multimedia content. For example, a case study scenario built as an e-learning course with quiz questions can be integrated into the record-keeping functions of an LMS or website because SCORM files follow a standard protocol. Proprietary e-learning software, like Tech-Smith Camtasia, Articulate Storyline, and Adobe Captivate (listed from the gentlest learning curve to the steepest), is capable of rendering SCORM files. Most often SCORM files are rendered as zip files that are recognizable by LMSs or websites; they allow users to interact with content, tracking results if tracking is desired. If assessment tracking is not necessary, the zip files can be uploaded to the instructor's website and linked or embedded in an LMS. Figure 4.5 shows a SCORM file displayed on a web page. Navigation at the bottom of the player allows learners to interact with the content presented.

There are several inexpensive web hosting services available; you will want a Secure Socket Layer (SSL) certificate so that your website can communicate securely with an LMS or other sites. Some e-learning software will have an FTP upload feature to send rendered e-learning files directly to your website. Other e-learning software zip files have to be uploaded directly. For example, after logging into my hosting account, I can upload files directly in the following manner:

1. Access the file manager.
2. Create a new folder for the e-learning files as shown in Figure 4.7.
3. Enter the folder and upload the files (typically it is a single zip file).
4. Locate the zip file and extract it. If the file exceeds hosting limits, try a third party tool like Filezilla for direct FTP upload. A screenshot tutorial is provided in Figure 4.8.
5. From the extracted files, locate the .htm or .html files as shown in Figure 4.9.
6. The address or URL for the file is domainname.com/foldername/filename.htm (or .html) as shown in Figure 4.10.

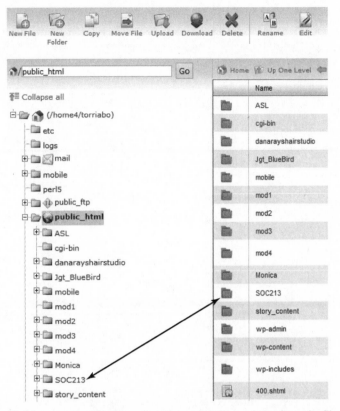

Figure 4.7 Folder created in file manager contains e-learning zip file

7. With the URL, you can share the file through various communication channels, including the iframe to embed into a learning management system, as shown on page 74.

USING MULTIMEDIA FOR ASSESSMENT

How do we know that learners have achieved the learning outcomes we set for them? How do we communicate assignment expectations to them and provide feedback along the way to their achieving a learning outcome? If a course or training requires learners to have an existing skill set prior to beginning a course, how is it assessed? It's important for students to know

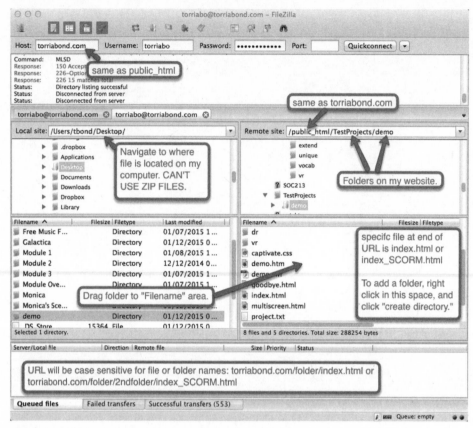

Figure 4.8 E-learning zip file extracted

how their work will be evaluated, and it's equally important for instructors to communicate their expectations and assess students throughout the instructional process. As with any course or training, a plan for assessment that is aligned with stated goals and objectives will ensure that outcomes for the course or training are achieved.

The design of an assessment plan is concerned with measuring the attainment of learning outcomes in an authentic context that emphasizes the cognitive skills of analysis, synthesis, and evaluation. As such, multiple types of assessments are evident in exemplary courses, including diagnostic, formative, and summative assessments. Diagnostic assessments determine what students know when they enter a course or training so

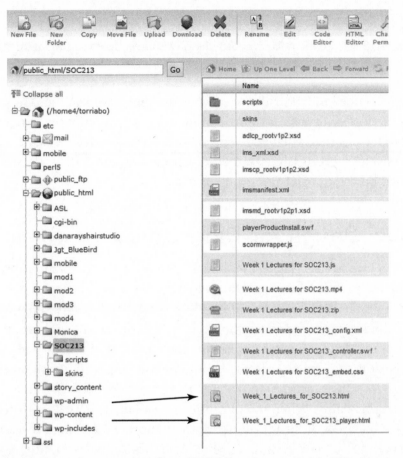

Figure 4.9 From the extracted files, the html web page is identified and used to create the URL

that the instructor can address misconceptions or biases regarding the content. Formative assessments help instructors know if learners are understanding prerequisite knowledge that leads to the final learning outcome. Summative assessments determine whether or not the final outcome was achieved. Through self-assessments, learners are also taken on this same journey to ensure that prerequisite learning objectives on the way to the final learning outcome are achieved. Self-assessments support learner autonomy and choice as they measure their progress toward learning outcomes. "Because any one assessment is imperfect and imprecise, collect

Figure 4.10 E-learning file created using Camtasia uploaded to instructor website

more than one kind of evidence of what students have learned. The greater the variety of evidence, the more confidently you can infer that students have indeed learned what you want them to" (Suskie, 2009). Instructors can assist learners in self-assessment by providing rubrics, checklists, and detailed descriptions of assessment criteria.

Visual Design for Diagnostic Assessment

Often in face-to-face classes I will begin a new unit with an attention-getting exercise. It might be a clip from a movie, a recent event in the news, a moral dilemma, a social problem, a case study, or a simulation. Many times responses and reactions are posted on chart paper around the room or on the whiteboard as relevant contributions are made. I always feel the attention-getting activity should provide me with information I can use to deliver instruction. For example, what do students know before instruction begins? What misconceptions do students have about the topic? What areas of the topic interest them most? Modifying the lesson in response to these questions is what makes the same lesson different, dynamic, and engaging for the instructor every time it is taught. It deter-mines what part of the lesson I can briefly mention and what part I need to deliver more methodically. Addressing the source and context of mis-understandings encourages critical thinking and reflection. To encourage independent exploration, resources can be provided for areas of interest that may not be part of the lesson.

How does an instructor or trainer get learners in an asynchronous course primed for a topic while simultaneously learning relevant infor-mation that influences instructional delivery? Sandra Bennet, an instruc-tional designer for online learning and an adjunct instructor for the College of Education Graduate Elementary Studies, K–6, at Wilmington

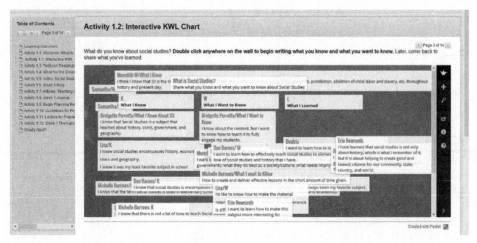

Figure 4.11 Interactive chart used as a diagnostic assessment, created using Padlet

University, takes advantage of an online bulletin board that can be linked and embedded into the course. Figure 4.11 illustrates a common diagnostic strategy referred to as KWL. The letters represent three ways to begin to engage learners in the lesson. K stands for finding out what learners *know* before the lesson begins. W recognizes that learners are further engaged by identifying what they *want* to know about the topic. And L notes that at the end of the lesson students reference what they knew and wanted to know from what they *learned.* If the instructor notices that aspects of what students wanted to know was not part of the lesson, the instructor has the opportunity to provide additional resources.

The web tool used to create the wall in Figure 4.11 is called Padlet. Students can asynchronously post and view comments made to the wall in real time. After creating a free account and logging in,

1. Click "create new padlet."
2. Type directions to the student on the padlet wall.
3. Locate the embed code and link to build padlet in your LMS or website.

Visual Design for Formative Assessments

If you've taught in a classroom for any length of time, you are probably familiar with the "deer in the headlights" look or the "lights are on but nobody's home" look. You know that facial expression on a student that says *I heard what you said but didn't understand the sense it made.* The good instructors among us will immediately recognize "the look" and pause the lecture or discussion to address questions. Needless to say, students taking courses online don't display the look. So how do we know they understand the instruction provided?

Checking for understanding before assessing a learning objective is an essential part of instruction. It gives the instructor an opportunity to reteach a concept if it was not fully understood or to provide additional resources to improve student performance. It can also give students an opportunity to revise an assignment and learn from their mistakes. Figure 4.12 shows the icons of learners who provided an auditory response to the question on the slide. The web tool used, called VoiceThread, allows instructors to facilitate verbal conversations around images, video, PowerPoint slides, and web links. This is one way to provide informal, low-risk formative assessment without increasing the number of papers you grade. After creating a free account and logging in, follow these steps:

1. Click "Create".
2. Click "Add Media."
3. Click the type of media you'd like to add (Figure 4.12 used PowerPoint slides adapted from the textbook publisher by clicking "computer" and searching for the PowerPoint file).
4. Repeat steps 1–3 until desired media have been added.
5. Narrate the slides, using the comment feature.
6. Locate the link and embed code for integration in an LMS or website.

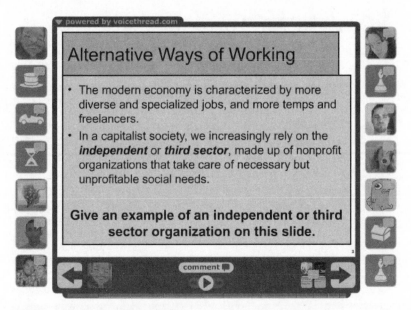

Figure 4.12 VoiceThread used as a formative assessment

Visual Design for Summative Assessment

Assignment rubrics are good tools for making grading criteria explicit to learners. An assignment rubric is an analytic rubric that measures student work according to several criteria. Students are made aware of not only the criteria but also the relative weighting of the criteria. The time invested in creating the rubric saves the instructor time in the grading process, as the description of achievement provides the justification for the evaluation. In this way, specific student feedback is minimized. Dr. Gretchen Bartels, an assistant professor of English for the Online and Professional Studies Division of California Baptist University, uses the rubric in Figure 4.13 to indicate to students they will be evaluated on four criteria. Two of the criteria are weighted more heavily than the others, which is made explicit using a rubric. Levels of achievement provide the feedback to students that explain

Criteria	Levels of Achievement	
	Exemplary	Accomplished
Oral Storytelling Weight 30.00%	90 to 100% The storyteller weaves the assigned elements and ending into a 4–8 minute oral story in the folktale and/or fairy tale tradition. The story shows excellent effort, creativity, and engagement.	75 to 89% The storyteller weaves the assigned elements and ending into a 4–8 minute oral story in the folktale and/or fairy tale tradition. The story indicates effort but less engagement than the exemplary story.
Reflection Weight 50.00%	90 to 100% The writer responds thoughtfully to the prompt and evidences strong engagement with the subject matter by answering a number of the questions posted in the prompt in depth.	75 to 89% The writer shows clear engagement with the assignment and oral storytelling; however, this engagement does not demonstrate as much depth as the exemplary level.
Commenting on Classmates' Blogs Weight 10.00%	90 to 100% In-depth, engaged comments are left on at least 3 classmates' posts.	75 to 89% Comments are left on at least 3 classmates' posts.
Mechanics and Style Weight 10.00%	90 to 100% The essay portion is flawlessly (or nearly flawlessly) written in strong and consistent academic style. Excellent word choice and sentence variety.	75 to 89% The essay portion is well written with a consistent academic style. Effective word choice and sentence variety; may include occasional repetition or other minor sentence-level errors.

Figure 4.13   Rubic shows relative weighting of evaluation criteria

the grade. While additional explanation may still be warranted, a rubric minimizes the need for extensive detail.

There are many ways to create an analytic rubric. Inserting rows and columns in a Word document is one way to create the cells for the achievement description. Building the rubric in a spreadsheet program is another way to create the rubric. Blackboard has a built-in feature for creating rubrics. The most challenging part of creating the rubric is identifying the appropriate verbiage to describe the levels of achievement. Many web-based rubric builders have a feature that allows you to search rubrics by keywords or subject areas. Viewing the language used in several rubrics can help you describe the range of achievement levels.

MULTIMEDIA FOR LEARNER ENGAGEMENT

When an instructor references engaging activities, typically it means that learners are actively involved in a task versus passively listening or observing. When we talk about an engaged student, we're referring to a learner who is intrinsically motivated to explore an area of interest (Conrad & Donaldson, 2004). Instructional multimedia appeals to a variety of learning styles and is appropriate for a variety of learning contexts. With the proliferation of free websites, independent exploration provides a social learning experience whereby learners can engage with content creators and gain access to instructional multimedia to support their intrinsic motivation to pursue a subject of interest. Courses can be built using the hierarchal page navigation on free websites as shown in Figure 4.14, which shows an excerpt of a course built on a Google Site by Michelle Procansky-Brock. The site is used to support a face-to-face online teaching workshop, with activities, videos, articles, and websites to explore outside of the workshop. After creating a free Google account, you are ready to build your own Google Site by following these steps:

1. Open the Google menu and click "Sites."
2. On the Sites page, click "Create."
3. Explore and select a website template.
4. Name your site and make other selections as desired or required.

Figure 4.14   Homepage of a course built on Google Sites

SCENARIOS

Recently I met with one of my colleagues, Dr. Monica O'Rourke, Assistant Professor of Kinesiology for the Online and Professional Studies Division at California Baptist University, who wanted to build an instructional scenario around a competitive sports and sponsorship dilemma encountered by an athletic director she knew. The dilemma would challenge students to wrestle with conflicts between the politics of meeting the needs and wants of athletic department faculty and ethical or moral decision making in the context of leadership and management styles. Through an instructional scenario, my colleague wanted her students to interact with course content in ways that foster the critical thinking skills of analysis, problem solving, evaluation, and reflection. While instructor-centered lectures and presentations can be pedagogically appropriate, student-centered approaches actively engage learners in problem solving, brainstorming, generating and responding to questions, debating, investigating, and collaboration. An instructor's understanding of the technology tools available through an LMS or website will enhance or hinder efforts to promote critical thinking through course design.

There are several ways an online instructor can build instructional scenarios on a website or in a learning management system. Consider the following ideas:

- The scenario and the relevant details can be written in a text document and posted on the website or in the LMS.

- Images and brief dialogue can be used to depict the scenario.

- The instructor can make a video explaining the scenario and the relevant details and post it in a discussion forum for critique or analysis.

These are all plausible options. However, they incorporate only one or two media. Another possibility is to add multimedia to the scenario. By integrating the three ideas mentioned with multimedia, you reduce the dependency on text, the inflection heard in the voice of the characters provides additional information, and the activity provides a multisensory learning experience.

If you're like me—a one-woman department—or a faculty member simultaneously building and teaching lots of courses, you may want to tackle the ultimate goal of building out multimedia scenarios in phases. This will allow you as an instructor to use the instructional scenario in a course while building and refining the scenario in each phase.

Phase 1: Write a scenario based on a real event, or find a well-written scenario through publisher resources or an internet search. Establish the scenario's context and variables that will influence the learners' decisions based on the learning outcomes and objectives of the course and lesson. Upload the document to an assignment submission area for student response.

Here is the instructor's scenario:

You are a university athletic director and have the final say on funding and spending. The remaining budget for the year is $400. You also just received a $5,000 grant that is allocated for fitness equipment for your strength and conditioning room, which all the sports teams share. The grant specifies the money is to be used only for fitness equipment—no exceptions. The coach of your championship men's basketball team is requesting all new basketballs for practices and games to replace the ones from last season. The coach of the women's cross-country team is requesting all new uniforms to replace the outdated and missing uniforms.

This past week a representative of the Galactica Energy Drink Company personally came into your office to thank you for letting their scantily clad "Galactica Energy Drink Girls" come to your sporting events unannounced and give free Galactica Energy Drinks to your athletes, students, and spectators. This was a surprise because you did not know this was happening. Before you could respond, the Galactica representative said she heard that you are in need of new uniforms for the women's cross-country team. In return for your willingness to allow their publicity stunt, she would like to offer you $20,000 to spend as you wish, a free unlimited supply of Galactica Energy Drinks for your athletes (with brand-new Galactica refrigerators in all your locker rooms and training rooms), and brand new Galactica Energy Drink logo uniforms for both the men's and women's cross-country teams. What do you do?

Choose only one response. Answer all the questions under either the "yes" or the "no" response.

If you say *yes* to Galactica:

- The cross-country coach has a big issue with making the athletes wear what the coach calls "porn uniforms." He is threatening to quit, and the season is about to start. He also mentions filing a lawsuit for a violation of Title IX, as the women have to wear new "porn uniforms" while the men do not. Your decision has been made (no wavering). Defend your decision and explain how you would respond to the coach.

- Athletes love the new drinks in the locker room—especially as it is an unlimited supply. Then the athletic trainer comes to you with this month's injury report, stating there has been a substantial increase in the number of athletes coming in with irregular heartbeat and palpitations and with extreme dehydration issues. In addition, he shows you two recent articles about deaths connected with energy drinks. If you pull out now, you will not fulfill the Galactica contract and will have to pay back the $20,000 and pay for the uniforms and all the drinks consumed. You've already spent the $20,000. What do you do?

If you decide to say *no* to Galactica:

- Explain two types of potential backlashes that may result when the coaches see all the new equipment for the strength and conditioning room, but no new uniforms. Explain how you plan to handle the fact that all the coaches know you, the athletic director, willingly turned down $20,000 plus "benefits" and that each coach's specific sports equipment needs still remain unmet? Describe two management or leadership strategies that could have been followed to prevent this from happening or how you now plan to handle this now that it has happened.

- The cross-country coach is a huge fan of Galactica Energy Drink and sees that you have squandered a potential sponsorship deal with a direct benefit of her team's getting new uniforms. The coach thinks you are out to get her. She decides to go over your head and files a complaint. The athletic board approaches you about her complaint about your violating Title IX. What do you do? Is the Title IX violation valid? Why or why not?

- CREDIT: Scenario contributed by Dr. Monica O'Rourke from Online and Professional Studies at California Baptist University

Phase 2: Storyboard the scenario. A storyboard is a rough sketch of images, characters, and dialogue that might be used in the scenario. Some instructional designers use PowerPoint to storyboard a scenario before it is built in an authoring tool with interactivity. Figure 4.15 shows eight slides that make up the storyboard for this scenario. The office pictures and characters were part of an e-learning subscription library. The images were saved as PNG files and uploaded into the LMS. Dialogue was typed above each image. At the first decision-making point, the last image is uploaded as an assignment, creating a repository for student's response, as shown in the final slide. The slides in Figure 4.15 make up the Phase 2 storyboard, which could be used in the next iteration of the course or training.

One way to create background images without a subscription service is to use a digital camera such as the camera on your smartphone. Today's smartphones come with awesome cameras. With decent lighting, I took a picture of an office cubicle and uploaded the image to PowerPoint. With the same smartphone, I took a picture of my colleague against a tan wall near her cubicle. After uploading the image to PowerPoint and using PowerPoint's background removal feature, I was able to place my colleague in the cubicle. Because of my learning curve with the background feature in PowerPoint, it took approximately thirty minutes to produce the image in Figure 4.16. (We are doing ourselves as professors and trainers an injustice if we use PowerPoint only to make linear bullet point presentations; it is capable of so much more.) Again, this is just one way to build a scenario to foster critical thinking and visually support it in an online course or training. You may be wondering why I would go through the effort to build each image separately in the LMS rather than uploading the PowerPoint file to the LMS and being done with it. Remember, images increase the file size, and some students may have difficulty with the download based on internet speed or other access issues.

Phase 3: Add multimedia to the scenario. Using the storyboard and an e-learning authoring tool, construct the scenario, integrating multimedia. One way to do this is to create a narrated screencast of the scenario, upload the video to a video hosting service, and embed the video in the LMS. Depending on the folder depth ratio planned for the instructional

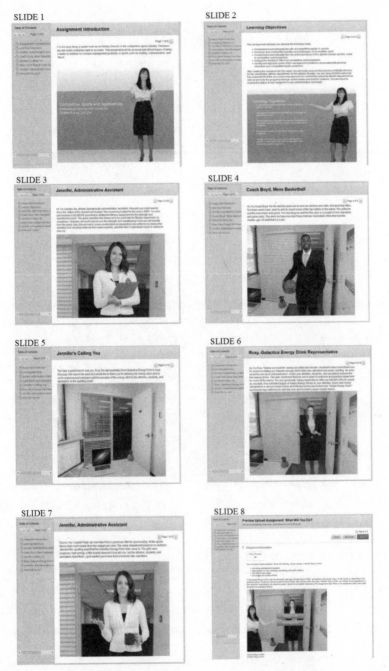

Figure 4.15 Storyboard slides used to create context for a learning scenario

Figure 4.16 Separate images of model and office scene; PowerPoint used to remove the model background and superimpose on office background

unit, this may be a good option. Alternatively, it is possible to add audio to slides in PowerPoint and convert the file to an MP4 video file for uploading to a video hosting service from which it can be embedded in an LMS or website. To convert a PowerPoint file to a video file, follow these steps:

1. In PowerPoint 2013, click "File".
2. Select Save As.

3. Navigate to the location where you want to save the video file.

4. Under Save as Type, select MPEG-4 video.

Branching Scenarios

Role-playing and simulations are some of instructors' favorite strategies to implement in traditional classrooms. Their use is supported by the Active Learning framework, which promotes high learner engagement in authentic and real-world situations. These strategies provide an opportunity for learners to practice the decision-making skills essential to the practitioners in a given discipline. With a little creativity, these strategies can also be implemented in the online environment.

You may recall that in Chapter Two it was suggested you start with what you know. Let's revisit our use of PowerPoint and YouTube. PowerPoint offers the unique capability to jump to particular slides in a presentation based on user input. Normally we use PowerPoint to make linear presentations: we begin at slide one and advance to slide two, then three, and so on. Being able to jump to slides out of order allows us to create interactive decision-making scenarios that are responsive to user decisions. This is often referred to as a branching scenario. Branching scenarios require students to make decisions at key points in the scenario, and the scenario continues based on the student's decisions. Figure 4.16 is one of twenty slides in a scenario created in PowerPoint. The slide shows a decision-making point in the scenario. Each choice is linked to continue the scenario based on the user's decision. Figure 4.17 shows how a hyperlink is used to jump to another slide in PowerPoint. Save the presentation as a PowerPoint show and it's ready to be uploaded to the LMS or website.

There are a couple of ways you could display the file in the LMS. You could upload the file and present it as a link. Students would click the link, and the file would download before it plays. You could also save the file to cloud storage and hyperlink the URL to an image. Students click the image, and the file downloads before it plays.

What if we want to add narration or additional video? If we do this in PowerPoint, the file size would be huge and impractical for downloading

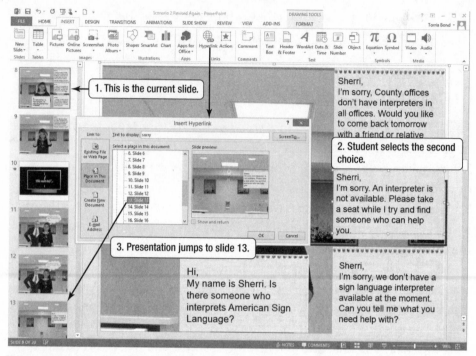

Figure 4.17 PowerPoint can be used to create nonlinear presentations responsive to user input

by students. However, we can leverage YouTube's hosting service and use the annotations feature to create hyperlinks for decision points. Here's what's possible. Using the PowerPoint scenario you created, screencast and narrate the scenario separately from each decision point. Upload each screencasted video to YouTube. Play the scenario. At the decision-making point, create hyperlinks to the videos that play out the user's choice, as shown in Figure 4.18. Once we've created the links to all the decision points in the scenario, we're ready to embed the beginning of the scenario in the LMS or website.

INTERACTIVE LEARNING OBJECTS

Several of my colleagues find the use of case studies a practical way of bringing real-world situations into the classroom. In the face-to-face

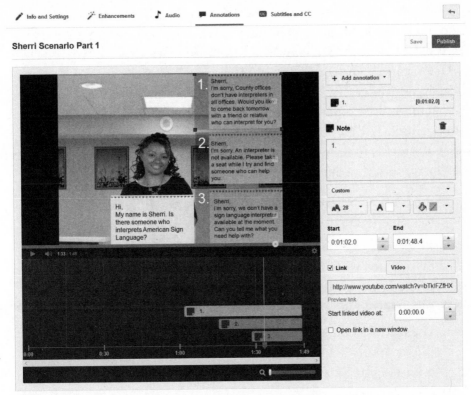

Figure 4.18 YouTube can be used to host videos of decision-making points in a scenario

classroom case studies might be distributed, read silently, and then discussed in small groups before the instructor guides the learning experience. While the online course can follow a similar agenda, a unique opportunity to infuse an interactive learning object presents itself to the online classroom. An interactive learning object is a container of instructional resources that require learner engagement to access. Learner engagement can be as simple as clicking the next button or as complex as responding to open-ended questions after reviewing resources contained in the object.

Typically, case studies are presented to learners in text format and they explore the complex circumstances around a specific organization or event. In collaboration with Professor Scott Dunbar, assistant professor of business of Online and Professional Studies at California Baptist University, I attempted to convert a Cirque du Soleil case study published by Delong and Vijayaraghavan (2002) into an interactive learning object. Although the interactive learning object is not complete at this time, the plan is to incorporate Cirque footage from YouTube, images of the founder and a few corporate staff, along with simulated documents and self-assessments to bring the case study alive visually. Professor Dunbar anticipates these benefits:

1. Students who have not seen a Cirque show will grasp the complexities of a production shown on multiple continents simultaneously.

2. Responses to basic comprehension questions about the case can be solicited with the learning object, and instructor insight can be offered through the feedback features of the authoring tool as a self-assessment.

3. The learner will be guided in the gathering and analysis of information about the influences on the case in preparation for a final assignment submission.

Figure 4.19 is a draft of one scene from the interactive learning object. The scene represents a floor plan of seven offices that simulate the location of key Cirque staff. The student clicks on the staff person's name to enter the office and "interview" the staff, who are representative of key positions in the organization (i.e. casting director, chief operating officer, choreographer, etc.) The floor plan in the figure was created on a design website. Homestyler. com is a site where you can design a room, add furnishings, and view the room in 3D or take a screenshot of the room in 2D for later use. Google "create a room design" or similar phrase to find a site. Creating a room is a great way to create backgrounds for an e-learning project. Once the screenshot in Figure 4.19 was created, it was uploaded to an author tool located at Smartbuilder.com. After creating a free account, view the sites tutorials to learn how to build interactions. The learning curve is well worth the investment of time.

Cirque Case Study

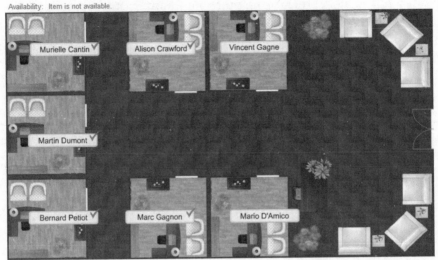

Availability: Item is not available.

Murielle Cantin ✓   Alison Crawford✓   Vincent Gagne

Martin Dumont ✓

Bernard Petiot ✓   Marc Gagnon ✓   Mario D'Amico

You have arrived in the lobby of the corporate office. Click on a name to enter the office and interview a corporate office staff. Interviewing staff in key positions will provide you with information to help you identify the core problem and secondary problem that hinder the effective management of 8 shows across four continents.

Continue

◀ 3 of 5 ▾ ▶

SB

Figure 4.19 Screenshot of floor plan incorporated into a learning object overlayed with buttons for interactivity.

SUMMARY

Multimedia is any combination of text, audio, video, images, graphics, animation, simulation and various types of interactive learning objects. The inclusion of multimedia begins with the readability and legibility of text and the hosting of multimedia files. Instructional assessments and learner engagement can be made visual through the use of web tools, SCORM files, branching scenarios, and interactive learning objects.

WHAT'S NEXT?

Practice displaying various types multimedia and identify ways you can use multimedia for instructional assessment and learner engagement. The types of multimedia content used in a course will depend on subject matter, teaching style, and learning outcomes, among other factors. Consider a course you are developing and do the following:

1. Design an assessment plan that integrates multimedia and includes diagnostic, formative, and summative assessments.

2. Use a table to format text and any combination of multimedia items.

3. Locate a scenario and create a storyboard for a branching scenario.

4. Build a branching scenario using an authoring tool of your choice, based on a storyboard of a scenario.

5. Establish your own website, then upload a SCORM file and display the file in your learning management system or website.

5

HOW DO I VISUALLY DESIGN A COURSE?

> Good design is obvious. Great design is transparent.
> —Joe Sparano, graphic designer and teacher

Let's pull together what we now know about visually designing a course in a learning management system (LMS) or website and integrate appropriate pedagogical practice. To do this, together we'll design a course that takes into account basic design principles, color selection, and combining of typefaces. At the same time, we'll illustrate how educational models of instruction can be combined with the L.I.T.E. skills for the visual design. Since this book is not about course development, I'm going to quickly gloss over the preplanning steps. I'm going to begin with a backward design planning model and briefly discuss my goals for developing an online design course for non-designers. Good visual design will be evident through the creation of instructor and peer presence, accessible course content, and the availability of instructional resources at the point of need. Undergirded by the Universal Design for Learning (UDL) framework, the course will initiate and sustain a welcoming online learning community among the participants and the instructor. It will use both the L.I.T.E. skills to visually design instructional content and the cautionary concept of avoiding a M.E.S.S., to ensure a low folder depth ratio and accessible instructional content with multimedia infused throughout the learning modules.

Because the professional development course will require participants to design a set of instructional content pages that exhibit basic design principles, a color scheme, and a combination of typefaces, we will use the inquiry model of instruction. The inquiry model of instruction is a classification of models that include problem-based, project-based, and other inquiry methodologies, rooted in the constructivist movement of the 1960s (Ornstein & Hunkins, 2009). The works of psychologists and educational researchers such as Piaget, Vygotskey, and Dewey are foundational to inquiry models of instruction (Conrad & Donaldson, 2004). This model is useful in helping students explore solutions to multifaceted questions. In this case, the questions or problem is how do you design a set of instructional content pages. The instructor in this model serves as a subject matter expert, not a conveyor of information; as such, the instructor provides resources for students to explore as they look for possible solutions to their questions. In addition, students are encouraged to generate their own questions and seek additional resources.

The various inquiry models of instruction contain four basic phases. First, there's the identification of a problem, such as how to design instructional content pages. Second, there is an exploratory element that includes books, blog posts, multimedia sources, and maybe scholarly journal articles. In this course, resources related to design principles, color selection, and typefaces will be explored. Third, possible solutions are generated. In this case, participants will consider multiple color schemes, combinations of typeface, and creative ways to apply the design principles. Lastly, a decision is made and applied. Some models of inquiry will include a reflection or evaluation element. In this course, reflection will be implemented separately from the inquiry model.

In each of the phases of the inquiry model, other models of instruction will be used as strategies to accomplish the goals of each inquiry element. For the purpose of describing the construction of this course, the term *instructional model* refers to pedagogical or andragogical processes that consist of research- or theory-based steps toward teaching skills, facts, and knowledge. The term *strategy* describes an approach to a given phase. For example, brainstorming is a strategy; a presentation is a strategy; discussion is a strategy. These are considered strategies because there are several techniques in instructor can use. For example, brainstorming can be done individually or in groups, verbally or in writing, in text or pictures. A presentation can be shared through lecturing, slide show, or dramatic performance. Discussions can be done through question and answer, Socratic dialogue, or debate. These are all techniques. Tools are materials used to facilitate the implementation of techniques. For example, group brainstorming online can be done on a shared Google Doc, a discussion forum, or an open-ended question presented through a polling web tool. A lecture can be made through a screencasted PowerPoint, or PowerPoint slides can be uploaded to a web tool and narrated. A debate can be crafted in a discussion forum or interactive web tool. Models of instruction, strategies, techniques, and tools will be seen throughout the course we develop together.

Content is king! This was stated earlier in Chapter One and bears repeating. It must be in the forefront of our minds when a course is designed. A good-looking course without equally good content is like being all dressed up with no place to go. That would be disappointing for both the learner and the instructor.

The learning outcome for participants will be to design a set of content pages that exhibit the four basic design principles, a specific color scheme, and a combination of typefaces. The course will be developed over four learning modules that address the following objectives:

- Identify four basic principles of design.
- Choose a color scheme.
- Combine fonts that work well together.
- Design a set of content pages.

Let's begin with module one. Module one will address the four basic principles of design. Those basic principles are introduced using two common instructional methods—concept attainment and concept development. These instructional methods serve the purpose of introducing foundational understandings in the language of the discipline and enabling learners to apply the foundational understandings in new settings. These models are associated with instructor-led face-to-face courses, so we will modify the traditional steps associated with these models for an asynchronous online environment.

Module One Lesson Objective: Given a variety of examples and non-examples, identify the four basic principles of design as noted by the author of the text.

This learning module uses two models of instruction to introduce the foundational elements of the course and apply those elements to the visual design of a set of content pages. The first model of instruction is referred to as concept attainment. The concept attainment model is based on the research of cognitive psychologists Jerome Bruner, Jacqueline Goodnow, and George Austin. Through the examination of exemplars, students isolate and identify concepts (Bruner, Goodnow, & Austin, 1967). The purpose of this method is to introduce a term or phrase, define that term or phase based on its attributes, and compare and contrast examples with non-examples so that the learner can identify the relationship between the term or phrase and its attributes. Two strategies are implemented in this model of instruction. The first is differentiating similarities from dissimilarities. The technique is the act of comparing examples and non-examples; the tools are images of the term or phrase that isolate the concept to be identified. The second strategy is brainstorming. The technique used is a small group setting in which ideas are written in text. The tool is an interactive wall, as shown in Figure 4.11 in Chapter Four.

This learning module also uses the concept development model of instruction. Based on the works of educator Hilda Taba (Gallagher, 2012), this model emphasizes inductive and independent thinking. As we conclude module one, we use the strategy of classification to develop the participants' ability to associate each of the four basic principles with the visual design of a set of content pages. The technique is the labeling of groups, and we continue to use the interactive wall as our tool. To do this we associate the basic principles of design to known settings, and then classify the associations in ways that ideally will lead to creative design ideas for content pages in an LMS or website.

On the outside of the module, I want to convey information about the unit to be studied: the learning objective, the title of the unit, and an image that embodies the learning objective. Although I could embed a video overview of the module, with text identifying the learning objective, I have chosen to simply use an image; there is no right or wrong, just

Module 1: Four Basic Principles of Design

Learning Objective: Given a variety of examples and non-examples, identify the four basic principles of design as noted by the author of the text.

Figure 5.1 Entrance to the learning module contains the learning objective, a unit title, and an image that relates to the unit objective

personal preference. Because I like to build on what I already know in order to manage the learning curve with new technologies, I have chosen to use a PowerPoint template to keep with a consistent color and layout theme. The images were selected using the Google search filter "labeled for reuse." Figure 5.1 is the result, and I'm happy with the look and feel.

As I enter the module, I have chosen to build upon what students already know about the four basic design principles of repetition, contrast, alignment, and proximity (Williams, 2008; Lohr, 2008) as it relates to choosing what to wear every day. To do this, I apply the concept attainment model to the identification of these basic design principles. Here are the steps of the concept attainment model that lend themselves well to the online environment:

1. As the instructor, I have to identify the concept(s) that I want learners to attain; in this case, the four basic design principles.

2. I also must already be able to define the concept and identify the attributes of the design principle.

3. I must gather examples and non-examples of the concept in images.

4. I must display the examples and the non-examples in a way that isolates the attributes of the example so that the single concept stands out (this is definitely the challenging part).

5. The students will compare the examples to determine commonalities that suggest a single concept.

I've chosen to build the concept attainment model using the test feature of Blackboard. Why? Several reasons, all of which have to do with avoiding a M.E.S.S.

Most students will be able to use the test feature intuitively. Written and verbal instructions will explain to students to click the "Click to Launch" link to begin the exam. After that, the features of the LMS prompt them what to do next.

By using the test feature, I can share a short video introduction about the context of the concepts and present examples and non-examples of each of the four concepts, without developing a folder and content for each concept. This keeps my folder depth ratio low. Initially, I created the module and then created a folder for each concept. It didn't take long for me to realize I had the makings of a M.E.S.S. if I continued in that way. In one content item, I can present and explain four concepts separately and distinctly. Students will view explanations of the concepts through the test feedback feature, whether they answer correctly or not. That's where part of the instruction is woven in.

I can streamline what could have been separate learning activities into one. This one activity helps introduce new concepts and allows me to diagnose and build upon what students already know about the concepts being introduced.

Because I'm using the test feature to present and assess the concepts, I have not mixed actionable items with items that require no action on the student's part. Having only actionable items minimizes opportunities for frustration and misunderstandings.

How did I build this lesson in an LMS, and how are the steps of the concept attainment model evident? First, I built the examples and non-examples in PowerPoint using the layout template for comparisons. Second, I chose to use the fill-in-the-blank test feature because each of the design principles happen to be one word (i.e., repetition, contrast, alignment, and proximity). In the text editor of the fill-in-the-blank test item, I uploaded the four PowerPoint slides containing the examples and non-examples. Putting all the images into the same test item, as shown in Figure 5.2, allows students to see all the examples and non-examples at one time and to study the images as long as they'd like. I chose to allow answers that I think come close to the concept. With experience teaching the course, I'll be able to add more correct answers based on the kinds of responses I receive when the course is taught. The feedback narratives explaining the concept will be shown whether their answer is correct or incorrect. This can be done in the LMS by entering the same text in the fields provided for feedback directed at correct and incorrect answers. I'll develop the remaining four concepts in the same manner.

Now that we've introduced the four basic design principles, we'll use what the students already know about them to develop the concepts in the context of visually designing a set of content pages. The instructional model we'll use—the concept development model—involves brainstorming, classifying, and synthesizing. To help learners apply the four basic design principles, we want to broaden their mental associations with each principle, to promote divergent thinking about each principle and the potential application to the design of a set of content pages. We will do this by

- Brainstorming as many associations as possible with each of the four principles of design
- Classifying the list of associations based on similar attributes
- Labeling the different classifications
- Merging the labels and list of associations under the labels, if applicable
- Synthesizing the information generated into generalizations related to designing a set of content pages based on the four principles of design

Figure 5.2 Test feature of Blackboard used to implement part of the concept attainment model of instruction

When facilitating the concept development method a significant amount of brainstorming as a strategy takes place. A small group will probably generate more ideas than a single individual. Therefore we will use small groups as a technique. There are a couple of ways to build small group brainstorming into this lesson. I could use the group feature to create a private space in which small groups can brainstorm. Using the group feature tool would add additional content to the course. Students would need to be shown how to access their group and group features for the activity. At this point in developing the course, I don't see myself using the small group configuration more than once, so it's probably not worth the additional content I'll have to add to explain how to use the group space and features. My second option is to use the discussion board tool. Brainstorming is a simple task, so I suspect I could get by with creating separate threads in which small groups of students could brainstorm. If I use this feature, I could have a separate thread to model my expectation for the assignment and perhaps embed a video presentation with content and grading criteria. Since I won't be using the group feature of Blackboard, I'll embed a Google Doc as a tool in a small table to use as a sign-up sheet. The embedding of the Google Doc will not require additional tutorial content, just a link to it in case it is not immediately visible to students. In this way, I'm avoiding a M.E.S.S. by not introducing new technology and by streamlining the content presentation, assignment expectations, and grading criteria into one discussion item. Figure 5.3 shows one way to design the content page in an LMS. Can you think of other ways the content might be displayed?

When students enter the discussion forum by clicking "Click to Launch" (which I'll remember to make explicit when I proofread the course build), they will see four forums. One forum says "click here FIRST"; it contains a link to a VoiceThread presentation and an interactive wall for brainstorming, classifying, and labeling ideas. The VoiceThread presentation guides them through the steps in the concept development model and allows them to become familiar with the interactive wall on which they will post their ideas in small group. Figure 5.4 shows how the VoiceThread presentation and the interactive wall might look using the discussion board feature. In this case, the VoiceThread presentation is not embedded on the page, so as not to clutter the content page in the LMS. A link to the presentation is provided so that the interactive wall is the focal point on the page. Figure 5.4 also shows what the interactive wall might look like after group brainstorming. Figure 5.5 shows the PowerPoint slides uploaded to the

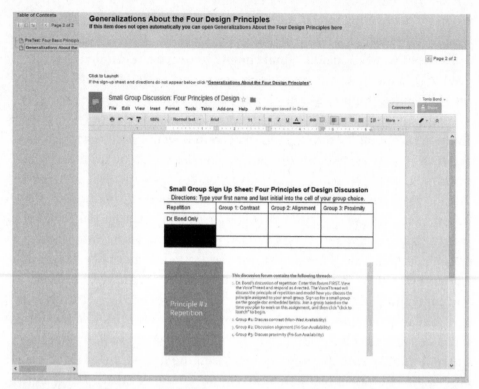

Figure 5.3 The iframe discussed in Chapter Three used to embed a Google document on the content page

VoiceThread; Figure 5.6 shows how the interactive wall might look after the classification and labeling. This allows students to practice posting ideas, moving the ideas around on the wall, and creating labels.

At this point in the lesson, students have signed up for small group; they've listened to the presentation (I hope) and practiced on the interactive wall. Now they are ready to brainstorm in their small group thread, which mirrors the look of the thread that contained the directions and the interactive wall on which they practiced.

The last step in the model is to review the list of ideas, classifications, and labels and make generalizations about the basic design principle assigned to the group that might have application to the visual design of a set of content pages. The VoiceThread presentation will model the expectation through the discussion of the basic principle of repetition. Students

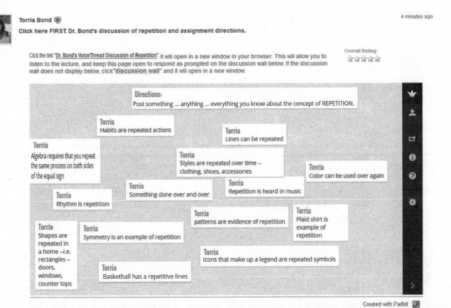

Figure 5.4 Interactive wall is the focal point of the content page, with links to instructor presentation and the interactive wall outside the Blackboard environment

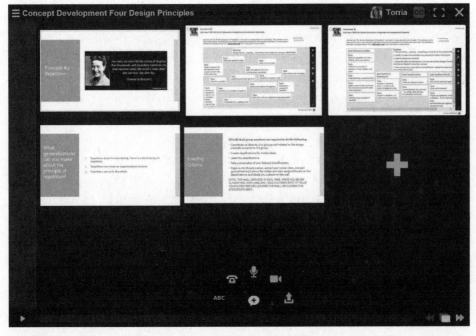

Figure 5.5 Instructor PowerPoint slides uploaded to VoiceThread, explaining the steps of the concept development model

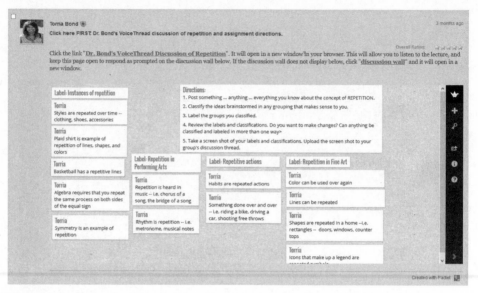

Figure 5.6 How the interactive wall might look after the classification and labeling exercise of the concept development model

will have seen my interactive wall and the classifications and labels I created. I will talk through the variety of settings I generated in which repetition occurs in my surroundings and explain how that led me to the generalization (and oxymoron) that there is a lot of variety in repetition. Repetition doesn't have to be the same thing over and over and over again. Often repetition is considered boring. However, in design repeated elements can contain originality or new content. For example, I can repeat discussion elements each week of a course. Having a discussion element based on the same kind of material—such as chapter text reading—might get pretty boring after the third week. However, I can repeat the element of weekly discussions using different media, such as an article on a current event or trend, a video, an image, a scholar in the field's blog post. When students finish brainstorming and generalizing with their small group, a group member is responsible for posting the best three generalizations on the design principle assigned, in preparation for the application of the design principles to a set of content pages. I encourage them to review the brainstorming and generalizing completed by the other groups. Because it is a professional development course, I would not build in accountability. I hope that the exercise will generate natural curiosity to inspire a review of the other groups' work. As discussed in Chapter Three, the advance preparation of the brainstorming space, including the disabling of additional threads, will keep related topics in the same space.

Module Two Lesson Objective: Given personal color preferences, select a color or color scheme that supports legibility in the design of a set of content pages in LMS.

In module two, we want participants to be able to select a color scheme to apply to the design of content pages in an LMS or website. The instructional model employed in this learning module, referred to as "into, through, and beyond," aids comprehension of discipline-specific language. The method is based on the work of Brinton and Holten (1997) and the phrase "into, through, and beyond" came out of the California Literature Project. The three phases of lesson planning for this model of instruction include

- Ascertaining what students already know or providing a common experience from which students can discuss what is already known

- Connecting what students already know to the new content

- Applying the new content to new situations

There are many strategies that can be used to ascertain what students already know about color selection or to provide a common experience from which students can discuss what is already known. Because we started module one by brainstorming what was known about the four basic design principles, let's provide a common experience from which students can discuss what is already known about color selection. Presentation of content is one possible strategy. Using a multimedia technique, participants could view a short embedded video (a tool) of an interior designer talking about selecting colors for the home. Using the technique of reading, students could analyze a blog post (a tool) by a retail manager discussing seasonal colors in a designer's clothing line. We could use the technique of question and answer to spark a discussion (strategy) about how course participants select colors for a planned event such as a Super Bowl party, kid's birthday party, or wedding. In this case, I've chosen to involve students in a survey about colors they enjoy, followed by a short video on the color wheel that will introduce them to key vocabulary. By the end of this "into" exercise, students should conclude that any color or color combination is workable, given appropriate brightness and contrast between neighboring elements.

This "into" activity could be built a couple of different ways. I could create a survey, embed the color wheel video, and create an assignment submission area for the questions, for a total of three content items. Knowing that I will have other content for the second and third phase of this model, I have chosen to create a survey. The survey will contain five items. The first four questions will concern colors they enjoy. The fifth question will have an embedded video introducing content-specific vocabulary, structured approaches to choosing color schemes using the color wheel, and a short answer submission area for responses to questions on how color affects us. Figure 5.7 shows how the activity was built using the survey tool in Blackboard. The survey settings display each question one at a time to ensure the video is viewed after the questions have been answered.

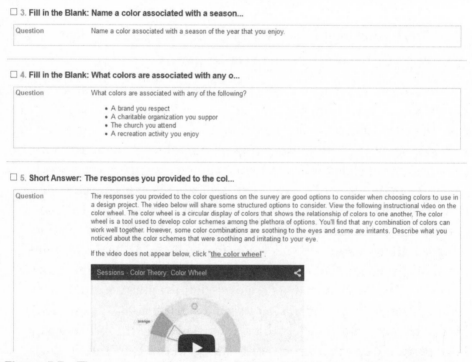

☐ 3. **Fill in the Blank: Name a color associated with a season...**

Question	Name a color associated with a season of the year that you enjoy.

☐ 4. **Fill in the Blank: What colors are associated with any o...**

Question	What colors are associated with any of the following?
	• A brand you respect
	• A charitable organization you suppor
	• The church you attend
	• A recreation activity you enjoy

☐ 5. **Short Answer: The responses you provided to the col...**

Question	The responses you provided to the color questions on the survey are good options to consider when choosing colors to use in a design project. The video below will share some structured options to consider. View the following instructional video on the color wheel. The color wheel is a circular display of colors that shows the relationship of colors to one another. The color wheel is a tool used to develop color schemes among the plethora of options. You'll find that any combination of colors can work well together. However, some color combinations are soothing to the eyes and some are irritants. Describe what you noticed about the color schemes that were soothing and irritating to your eye.
	If the video does not appear below, click "the color wheel".
	Sessions - Color Theory: Color Wheel

Figure 5.7 The survey tool is used to elicit students' known color preferences for possible use in color selection when designing content pages in the cumulative assignment

The next phase of the model provides students with hands-on experience with the new content. The "into" phase introduced students to terminology: hue, tint, shade, warm colors, cool colors, complementary colors, triads, split complement triads, and analogous colors. "Through" activities might include case studies, scenarios, simulations, role-playing, or reading guides as strategies. For example, we could present students with a floor plan of a bedroom (a tool) and a designer's rationale for the color choices. Participants could analyze the designer's color choices, using the vocabulary introduced through the video presentation. We could use a scenario as a strategy and present the student with a profile of a client (a tool) who wants to redesign their home. We could use role-playing as a strategy by having the student play the role of a party planner and choose a color scheme for a backyard poolside reception.

Because the students will take what they learn about basic design principles in clothing, and color selection in furnishings, and transfer that knowledge to the design of a set of content pages, I have chosen to embed a room design simulation (a strategy) in the course. Manipulating colors in a room design will allow students to visually see color contrast and brightness and feel the impact color has on us. Why is this so important? Have you ever been given a six-page document in Times New Roman with all the text in royal blue? What about a PowerPoint presentation with light yellow text on an off-white background? Or worse yet, a neon green PowerPoint slide with neon pink capital letters in Old English font? (OK, I'm exaggerating a little.) Ideally, by manipulating the wall colors in a room simulation and seeing the impact of color combinations, the participants' design of their own content pages will reflect decisions that positively impact readability, legibility, and recall. Figure 5.8 shows the embedded simulation from a website. Since the website containing the simulation did not provide an embed code, the iframe discussed in Chapter Three was used to embed the website in the LMS.

The last phase of this model is "beyond." The purpose of "beyond" activities is to provide opportunities for creative expression of the newly learned content. In this case, participants are being asked to go beyond the clothing and furnishings context and apply the new content to the design of content pages in an LMS. To accomplish this, guided simulation

Figure 5.8 Color exploration simulation from a website embedded in the content page using the iframe from Chapter Three

questions (a tool) with a submission area for reflection (also a tool) culminates this phase of the instructional model. Figure 5.9 shows a PowerPoint slide image with guided simulation questions. On this content page, students have access to the slide as a PowerPoint file for enhanced accessibility. In addition, I provided a link to the instructional video on the color wheel for review and quick access.

Module Three Lesson Objective: Given the differences among typefaces, select a combination of typefaces to promote readability on a set of content pages in the LMS.

The basic elements of a typeface are as multifaceted as the task of designing a set of content pages. Because of this, I've chosen to use the same inquiry-based model of instruction with this module. Module one sets up the question for how to design a set of content pages in an LMS. Modules one, two, and three are part of the exploratory phase of the model; module three, however, applies all four phases of the inquiry model in this one unit. In module three, we want students to select a combination of typefaces to use throughout a set of three content pages. Type is the building block of print communication. Therefore, it is essential

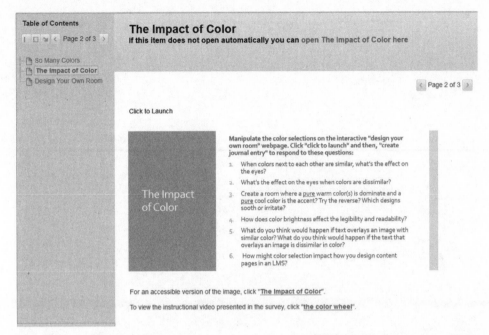

The Impact of Color
If this item does not open automatically you can open The Impact of Color here

Page 2 of 3

Click to Launch

The Impact of Color

Manipulate the color selections on the interactive "design your own room" webpage. Click "click to launch" and then, "create journal entry" to respond to these questions:

1. When colors next to each other are similar, what's the effect on the eyes?

2. What's the effect on the eyes when colors are dissimilar?

3. Create a room where a pure warm color(s) is dominate and a pure cool color is the accent? Try the reverse? Which designs sooth or irritate?

4. How does color brightness effect the legibility and readability?

5. What do you think would happen if text overlays an image with similar color? What do you think would happen if the text that overlays an image is dissimilar in color?

6. How might color selection impact how you design content pages in an LMS?

For an accessible version of the image, click "The Impact of Color".

To view the instructional video presented in the survey, click "the color wheel".

Figure 5.9   Guided questions from the higher level of Bloom's Taxonomy facilitate the color exploration simulation

for participants to distinguish (1) the differences between fonts and typefaces, (2) how typefaces differ among each other, and (3) which combinations of typefaces and formatting enhance readability. These are the three problems explored in this module.

Inquiry models require the instructor to serve as a content area expert for students. In this role, the instructor poses questions and suggests resources to help students construct a variety of solutions and ultimately to execute a decision. Research is the strategy used to acquire the information needed, and a graphic organizer is the tool used to record the findings of the participant's inquiry of selecting typefaces. The chart was built in Microsoft Word and contains active links to resources for students to explore. In Blackboard, the chart is copied and pasted into the text editor of the assignment feature for ease of use, access to hyperlinked resources, and a place to submit the completed assignment. A copy of the chart is provided to students in the same assignment area as depicted in Figure 5.10.

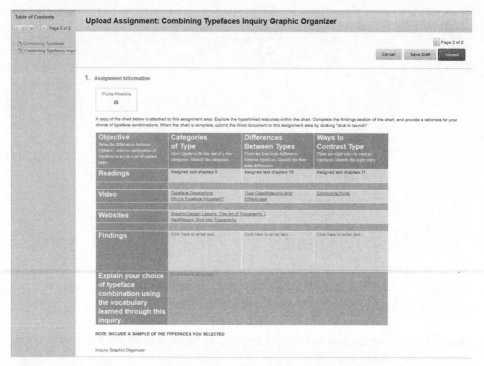

Figure 5.10 Graphic organizer used to facilitate independent exploration

In the same module area is a mini lecture combined with an explanation of the assignment. The template used to create the mini lecture is a free PowerPoint template with hyperlinked tabs that allow the presentation to be viewed sequentially or nonsequentially as needed. While Figure 5.11 shows the presentation being used as a mini lecture, this template can also be used to create real world scenarios with hyperlinked tabs that are responsive to user decisions. There are many free PowerPoint templates available online. Several PowerPoint online communities allow their templates to be freely downloaded; they can be found by googling "scenario PowerPoint slides free" or some variation of that phrase.

Module Four Lesson Objective: Given the four basic design principles, a color scheme, and a combination of typefaces, design a set of three content pages for an online course.

In this module, the last phase of the inquiry model, "decision," is completed. The student is asked to design a minimum of three instructional

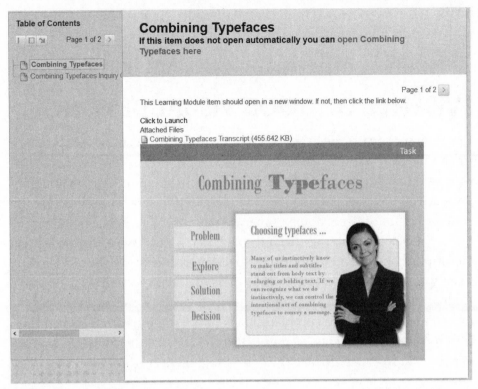

Figure 5.11 Introductory image slide of narrated instructor presentation with transcript provided

content pages. Using a narrated presentation strategy, students will explain their design choices, applying all that they have internalized about design principles, the use of color, and the use of typefaces. Students select a software application or web tool of their choice to narrate and present the set of instructional content pages they designed. The presentation format allows for reflection on the decisions made in the inquiry model of instruction that is shared with peers, inviting their reactions and insight to the design choices made. Reflecting on peer feedback serves as a springboard for revision and improvement at a later time. Because each student will display a set of content pages, the submission area provided uses the blog space. The blog space is an individual's editorial space to share their work and the rationale behind their decisions. The comments feature on each individual's blog page allows for peer reactions and insight. This allows the class to benefit from the creative ideas of its peers, and the individual student has a larger audience than the instructor from whom to receive feedback.

EVIDENCE OF GOOD VISUAL DESIGN

Now that we have created the content for this course, let's turn our attention to the evidence of good visual design mentioned in Chapter Two. There we stated that good visual design shows itself through instructor and peer presence, content accessibility, and instructional resources provided at the student's point of need. Some of the ways a sense of presence is shown include a welcome message from the instructor, intuitive navigation, and an introductory forum to encourage peer interactions. We should see a variety of media used in standard formats to ensure accessibility for all students across desktop and mobile devices. Lastly, we should see everything a student needs to complete a task in the same area where the task is introduced, so students need not click throughout the course to find a needed resource. Let's review the course together.

Creating Presence

Recently, a friend of mine moved into a new apartment and invited me over to hang out. When I arrived, my friend greeted me with a big smile and a hug and immediately began showing me around the apartment, of which she was very proud. When students enter this professional development module, I want to greet them in the same way (minus the hug). So I've chosen to make the landing page and the navigation pages the same, with quick access links to the learning modules on the course menu as shown in Figure 5.12. The welcome message is the entry to module zero, which contains a repurposed image of the professor, a screencasted orientation to the course in Blackboard, a screencasted overview of the course and its projects, and a participant introduction forum. Presence is also created throughout the learning modules, as participants brainstorm with one another in module one activities and post the content pages they design in module four.

Figure 5.12 Landing page and navigation page are the same, with quick access links to learning modules on the course menu

Accessible Content

Sometimes when I'm searching for information on the Web, I come across broken links. The URL can't be found or a file cannot be opened. I'm sure you've experienced a slight irritation when this happens (to put it mildly). Imagine what it must feel like for students using assistive devices or students who are deaf or hard of hearing when content in a course is not accessible (i.e., they can't hear the instructor's narrated lecture, or URL's are pasted in the course and the screen reader proceeds to read each character in the URL instead of a hyperlinked name of the URL). While closed captioned lectures and video are needed for deaf or hard of hearing students, they are not the only students who benefit from closed captions. Closed captions help learners whose first language is not the language of instruction. They help students studying in noisy spaces—like student athletes studying in a gym during a game. It would be ideal for all multimedia to be closed captioned in a course. However, it's not always possible to do so as a matter of practice without a qualifying student with approved accommodations enrolled in the course. Therefore it is a good practice to provide transcripts in standard Microsoft Word and PowerPoint file formats for multimedia used and images that contain alt text describing them. This allows all students to access course content from desktop and mobile devices. Remember, accessible content helps everyone.

Resource Availability

You've probably never done this, but there are times when I start a task and I don't have everything I need to complete the task. Such as the time when I was cooking a dessert and had forgotten to purchase the eggs I needed. Or the time when I prepared a cooking lab for middle school students and forgot to set out the chocolate chips needed for their chocolate chip cookie recipe. Lack of preparedness causes inefficiency in the work flow and increases the time it takes to complete the task. When it comes to course design, it is important to build the resources needed to complete a task in the same space where the task is introduced. For example, lectures are embedded in the content page for learner convenience. A link to the same lecture is provided just in case the embedded content is not visible. In module two, in which a simulation activity is required, students are not asked to go to another location to find the assignment simulation. Instead, the assignment simulation is embedded in the content page and a link is provided to the simulation's location on the Web if needed. In module three, there are several videos and websites to explore. All of those resources are provided in the same space where the completed assignment will be submitted.

SUMMARY

There are many right ways to build an online course or training, given aligned learning outcomes, instructional materials, and assessments. The course we built together models attempts to make the reasoning behind the visual design choices explicit. The distinction between educational models, strategies, techniques, and tools provide a common language by which we discussed many pedagogical and androgogical approaches to the presentation of instructional material. After the course was built in the LMS, we highlighted the evidence of good visual design, specifically how instructor and peer presence was created, how content was made accessible, and how resources were made available.

WHAT'S NEXT?

Now it's your turn to apply the L.I.T.E skills to avoid a M.E.S.S. in an online course that you create or revise. Practice integrating these ideas into a professional development course of your own.

1. Use a backward design planning model to identify or create an exemplar that illustrates what participants will be able to do when they complete the course or training.

2. Create learning outcomes and lesson objectives based on the exemplar you identified or created.

3. Create a rubric to describe the successful learning outcome. Table 5.1 is an example of the rubric I could start with for the professional development course we created together.

4. Given the learning outcomes and objectives, identify educational instructional models to use to help you logically sequence the instruction.

5. As you prepare the instructional materials, learning activities, and images, build the components of the course in an LMS or website using the L.I.T.E. skills, the design principles, a color scheme, and a combination of typefaces.

Table 5.1 Sample rubric for the cumulative activity, designing a set of content pages

	LEVELS OF ACHIEVEMENT		
CRITERIA	**EXEMPLARY**	**ACCOMPLISHED**	**MARGINAL**
DESIGN PRINCIPLES	**50 Points** The three content pages illustrate appropriate use of all the following: 1. Contrast 2. Repetition 3. Alignment 4. Promixity	**45 Points** The three content pages illustrate appropriate use of most of the following: 1. Contrast 2. Repetition 3. Alignment 4. Promixity	**35 Points** The three content pages illustrate inappropriate use of most of the following: 1. Contrast 2. Repetition 3. Alignment 4. Promixity
COLOR SCHEME	**25 Points** A consistent color scheme is applied across all three required content pages.	**20 Points** A consistent color scheme is applied across over half of the required content pages.	**15 Points** A consistent color scheme is applied acoss less than half of the required content pages
FONT COMBINATION	**25 Points** Fonts selected complement one another and have contrast for readability and legibility.	**20 Points** Fonts selected complement one another and have some contrast for readability and legibility.	**15 Points** Fonts selected may complement one another and lack of contrast hinders readability and legibility.

6

HOW DO I SUPPORT LEARNERS ONLINE?

Learners come from all walks of life—the rich and the poor, the emotionally healthy and the ill, the socially competent and the awkward, with high self-esteem and with low self-esteem. It's very common for learners to experience a variety of stressors while they are pursuing a course of study—births and deaths, weddings and divorces, caring for special needs children or elderly parents, recovering from addictions or traumatic experiences, managing successes and failures, purchasing and learning to use personal computers, tablets, and other mobile devices, or sending their computer for service to remove a virus or replace a hard drive that crashed. While some give up their pursuits during challenging times, many press on toward completion. And on top of those stressors, they've chosen to pursue a course of study that includes classes online in an age where the advances in technology are changing so rapidly that an online course of today is drastically different from an online course of five years ago. As we conclude the topic of visual design for online learning, it's important to integrate support for learners into online courses so that the educational experience is the focal point of the course and not just another stressor on learners' journey to success.

What does learner support look like in an online course? When a learner enters my online class, I want them to feel that the online space was prepared with them in mind. A prepared course ensures that students are able to find answers to all their questions and are aware that I am available to assist them when needed. The support needed to be success-ful in the online space is similar to the support needed by students in a traditional classroom. For example, on the first evening of a face-to-face class, the instructor reviews the syllabus. This might include a review of assignments, requirements outside of physical class time, and required text and materials. Many syllabi also highlight important institutional policies like academic integrity and the process of requesting an incomplete. During this time students can ask clarifying questions.

The need to understand the context of the class and to ask questions is the same for students taking a course online. The difference is that the physical availability of the instructor is limited or nil, and to avoid a delay in students accessing the resources needed, instructors have to anticipate students' needs before the online course begins. Learner support can include an explanation of course information and tutorials that explain required technology, where to access technology assistance after hours, instructor information, parameters affecting instructor response time, and assignment feedback. The resources provided should ensure that all learners have equal access to course content and have the opportunity to provide anonymous feedback throughout the course. The remainder of this chapter will address questions that students ask most often after they've arrived at the course landing page and suggests visual designs that contribute to the support needed.

WHERE IS THE SYLLABUS

I know professors often wonder whether or not students actually read the carefully crafted document known as the course syllabus. In Google Images, type the phrase "it's in the syllabus" and you'll see many satirical memes, cartoons, and T-shirts that convey an instructor's heartbreak when they're e-mailed questions like "What textbook do I need?" or "When is it due?" or "Can I turn it in late?" Rest assured, most students read the syllabus—and in their defense, some of our syllabi are becoming as long as the escrow papers you sign for your first home. In that situation, all you know is if you don't initial here and sign there, you won't get the keys to the front door. I realize how important it is to include all relevant institutional, school, department, program, and course policies in the syllabus. Nonetheless, what a student wants to know is not always easy to find.

The syllabus is the first document most students look for in an online course. How does an instructor make sure that important information is easy to find and the syllabus can be read by all students, including those who use assistive technologies? Dr. Dirk Davis, academic dean for the Online and Professional Studies Division at California Baptist University, specializes in distance education for working adults and others who need a flexible learning schedule. In collaboration with division administrators and faculty, he supported the design and distribution of an accessible syllabus template created in Microsoft Word.

When you create the syllabus in Word, highlight the section titles and apply style headings as shown in Figure 6.1. Doing this not only makes the syllabus accessible to students using screen readers but also creates a clickable table of contents in the navigation pane that students can scan to find specific information. When displaying the syllabus in a learning management system (LMS), use the heading styles available in the text editor, as shown in Figure 6.2. Although the options may be fewer than in a word processing program, they do allow screen readers to jump from one heading to the next, contributing to the accessibility of the entire syllabus. While attending the BbWorld 2014 conference, I attended a workshop on accessible design with Katie Evans and colleague. Katie is a manager of e-learning instructional design and quality assurance at Lake Sumter State College in central Florida. During the workshop she shared a browser add-on called Fangs Screen Reader Emulator. Once it's downloaded onto your browser, you can display a text version of the webpage similar to how a screen reader would read it, as shown in Figure 6.3. The text version of the web page shows how the screen reader summarizes the content of the page based on style headings and how each style heading is read before the heading title. This is why style headings are so important to those using assistive devices like screen readers. Style headings enhance the overall navigation of the document.

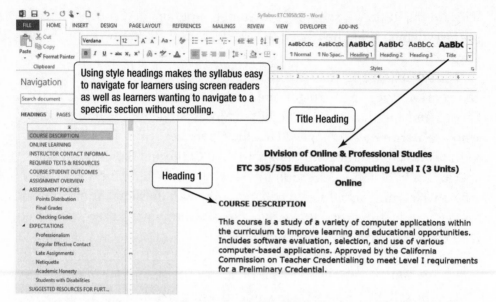

Figure 6.1 Microsoft Word style guides enhances document navigation for those using assistive devices and for those looking for specific content

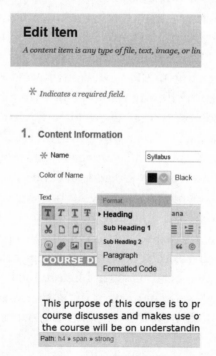

Figure 6.2 Use headings in text editors whenever possible to enhance navigation through large amounts of text

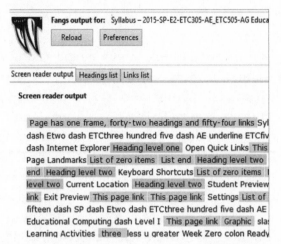

Figure 6.3 Text version of student view of course syllabus in Blackboard rendered with the Fangs Screen Reader Emulator browser add-on

If you have a syllabus document created in Microsoft Word 2013 that is not accessible, follow these steps to create leveled headings:

1. Highlight the title of the document.

2. Click the title style option located in the Styles grouping of the "Home" tab.

3. Highlight the title of the first major section.

4. Click the Heading 1 option located in the Styles grouping of the "Home" tab.

5. Highlight the title of subsections and click the Heading 2 option.

6. Additional style options are available in the Document Formatting group of the "Design" tab.

HOW DO I CHECK MY GRADES?

Next in importance to finding the syllabus, most students want to know how they will be graded and where can they find instructor feedback on assignments. Face-to-face courses offer multiple avenues for inquiring about one's progress. Students can show up early to class and ask for explanations on graded assignments. They can stay after class to review a concept privately with the instructor. Physical papers are regularly submitted, graded, and returned.

Online classes also have multiple avenues for checking one's progress. The assessment features in LMSs vary, so students need to be informed how to access their grades and other forms of instructor feedback. If an LMS does not use assessment features or is limited in those offered, the instructor needs to develop a system for communicating grades and assignment feedback. Several web-based tools allow instructors to maintain grading records, while allowing students to log in to view their grades and instructor feedback. A Google search on the term "grade book" will return several results. Figure 6.4 is from a screenshot tutorial of the student's grade view in Blackboard. The screenshot tutorial highlights how to access scored rubrics and points earned out of the total for the course, and the current letter grade. In addition, it highlights three possible areas

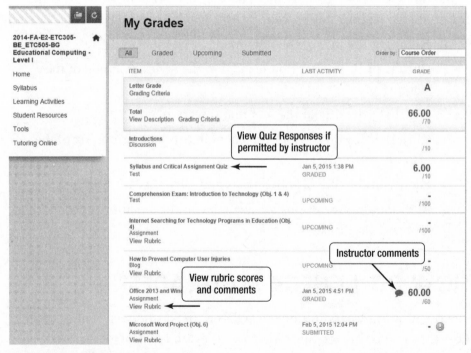

Figure 6.4 Screenshot tutorial for students showing how to access grades and instructor feedback

where students might find instructor feedback: the location for comments, scored rubrics, and quiz results.

HOW DO I CONTACT THE INSTRUCTOR

Instructor presence is an essential component of any course delivered fully online. Learners need to know that there is someone "on the other end of the computer" who is leading their educational experience, concerned about their achievement, and willing to connect with them in a timely manner. Simply providing your name, office location and hours, and contact number does not convey a sense of your being there for students. In contrast, a combination of text and a photo (smiling, please), with audio or video, presents the instructor as personable and approachable. Instructor contact information should be in a prominent place in the course, such as the course menu or entry to instructional modules.

There are many ways to combine an image, text, and video. For example, Figure 6.5 introduces Dr. Jason Rhode, director of the Faculty Development and Instructional Design Center at Northern Illinois

Figure 6.5 Arrangement of multimedia on the content page to facilitate contact with the instructor

University, where he oversees all faculty development. Notice how he arranged the instructor photo, video introduction, and contact information on the content page. This is done by saving the photo, text, and video to the same content item. (For tips on how to embed multimedia content in your courses, see Chapter Four.)

HOW DO I GET TECHNOLOGY HELP?

Students work on assignments at all hours of the day and night. If you've taught an online course and noticed the time stamp of student e-mails, you know they need help in the wee hours of the morning, when you're asleep, or during the business day, when an adjunct professor is working a full-time job. Typically, help requests are related to technology or course content: a student can't access a lecture video or needs clarification on assignment directions. During business hours, students can call the technology help desk or make an appointment with the instructor for assistance. However, many degree programs are designed for working adults, making it difficult for them to take advantage of resources offered during their work day. Therefore online instructors have to anticipate student help needs and provide for them in advance.

Jennifer Perkins, an instructional designer for Eastern Kentucky University's Online Instructional Development Center, supports faculty as they develop and design online courses. She has noticed a recurring technology help request: it's about web browser security features that block the visibility of insecure content in secured LMSs, thereby preventing students from viewing instructor-created YouTube videos and other content created with web tools. To inform learners how to handle this before they reach crisis mode, Perkins created a screenshot tutorial illustrating how to give the browser permission to display the content, shown in Figure 6.6.

Using your favorite screen capturing software, take a screenshot of what a panicked student will see when an instructional resource is not visible. Using text and square annotation features of the screen capturing software, identify where the browser communicates that content is blocked. In Figure 6.6, the designer has chronologically numbered the

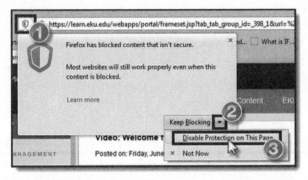

Figure 6.6 Screenshot tutorial showing how to release browser security when an instructor video doesn't display

steps to be taken to allow the blocked content to be displayed. A brief text explanation of why the video doesn't display and a text explanation of the steps to give the browser permission to display the video should accompany such an annotated screenshot.

HOW DO I GET HELP WITH ASSIGNMENTS

In addition to screenshot tutorials and help desk resources, students often need assistance with assignments in the late evening and early morning hours. Student-to-student forums contribute to the learning community of the course. This can be accomplished through learning management features such as the discussion board or blog tools. This can also be done using social media applications like Facebook or Twitter. Consider creating a private closed Facebook group just for students in your class to pose those late night and early morning questions to their peers, who probably are also working on the same assignment at these times. After creating a free Facebook account and logging in,

1. Click the Home link.
2. Click Create Group on the left sidebar.
3. Complete the fields in the "Create New Group" dialog box as shown in Figure 6.7.

Figure 6.7 Private Facebook group for late night and early morning peer-to-peer assistance

HOW DO I USE SPECIFIC COURSE FEATURES

Unless students move together as a cohort, it's very likely that each course you teach online will have at least one learner who is both new to the institution and new to learning online. This is particularly true if your institution has year-round open enrollment. How can an instructor help new students learn to navigate the course? Dr. Jenny Yeo, associate clinical lecturer, and Lynne Rawles, faculty of medical sciences e-learning coordinator, from Newcastle University, Newcastle upon Tyne, UK, provide screenshot tutorials of the navigation environment. They use text and basic shapes to highlight the location and function of the navigation features of the course, including how to use the text editor for assignment submissions. Figure 6.8 is a screenshot of the course welcome page. The rectangle shapes with numbered boxes are drawn on top of the screenshot using a free web tool like Jing, a free screen capture

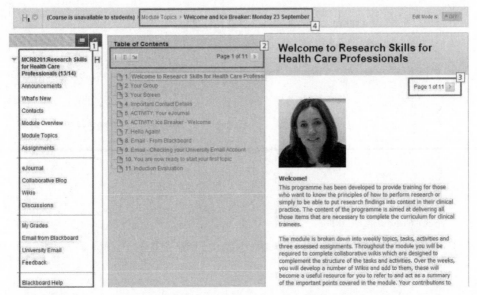

Figure 6.8 Screenshot tutorial explaining course navigation

software. Supporting text for the graphic would explain the following to students:

1. The course menu provides one-click access to featured areas of the course.

2. The table of contents contains clickable links to content in a learning module.

3. Page numbers in a learning module are navigable and help the learner gauge where they are in the topic material.

4. The "breadcrumbs" show students exactly where they are in relation to the course.

Produced using the same method as in Figure 6.8, Figure 6.9 is from a screenshot tutorial showing students how to use the text editor in the course to upload documents, images, and YouTube videos, and insert tables and links.

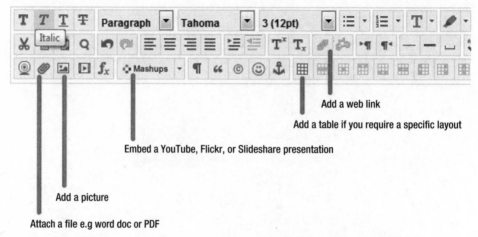

Figure 6.9 Screenshot tutorial explaining the use of the text editor

EPILOGUE: WHERE DO WE GO FROM HERE?

I entered the online teaching space in 2007, tasked with developing a hybrid course that would meet face-to-face four times over nine weeks, for four hours each night. Students loved the schedule; however, my colleagues and I remained skeptical about moving toward fully online classes. When I look back at my skepticism, I was most concerned about (1) not being able to convey my interactive teaching style online, (2) the problem of potential cheating and how to ensure the authenticity of student work submitted (as if those weren't already occasional problems in my face-to-face courses), and (3) student interaction and collaboration. I also had the habit of informally assessing student work through observation in the classroom and couldn't imagine how to transform looking over a student's shoulder to offering suggestions to the online space.

A significant portion of learning is social and occurs spontaneously when a peer challenges unspoken premises and presents alternative perspectives. I didn't like discussion board forums, initially. They were so overwhelmingly unmanageable. Who's going to read all those posts from peers, just to pick two people to respond to and earn ten out of a thousand points? Where's the critical thinking? As the instructor, do I really want to read all those posts, or am I using the grade tool just to count the number of comments made to peers and to award points? (Come on—I'm not the only one.) And from the student perspective, a conversation that would take thirty minutes in class now takes two hours to read through. The instructor doesn't know what's happening in the discussion forum, and it's the instructor's perspective on peer comments that students are most interested in.

In my role as an instructional designer and mentor to faculty teaching online, I have spent the last four years investigating online teaching practices, and collaboratively exploring ways to make the experience better for students and instructors. Today, I am 100 percent confident that learning online can be just as challenging, insightful, interactive, and collaborative as learning in courses delivered through any other medium. I also believe the visual design of content online is as important as the instructional content. Students are either emotionally engaged or turned off by the appearance of content online. Their sense of self-efficacy is affected by support or lack of support in using the online space. Because of the rapid changes in instructional design and educational technology in general, the ideas in this book are only a beginning point. Currently, there isn't much on the market to show how instructional content can be visually designed in a learning management system or website. More conceptual frameworks and images for visual designs are needed. How can mock trial style debates be visually designed in an LMS? How can literature circles be visually designed on a content page? What are some ways that behaviorist, constructivist, essentialist, existentialist, and post-modernist views of teaching might be visually displayed on the content page, and how would they differ from each other? In what other ways can direct instruction, discovery methods, and critical pedagogies be visually displayed online, and how would they differ from each other? Honestly, I don't have the answers to these questions, but I'm looking forward to reading a book by the next author who chooses to explore visual design for online learning.

Appendix **A**

SYLLABUS REVIEW SCRIPT

This appendix presents a sample script for reviewing the course syllabus in a screencast video. The script encourages students to read the syllabus in detail and reviews assignments and important course policies.

SYLLABUS REVIEW SCRIPT FOR SCREENCAST

The course syllabus is our contract regarding all aspects of this course. It contains important information and requirements that will help to ensure your success in the course. Take a few moments to review the course description and objectives on your own. Also notice my contact information and the required texts and resources for the course. You will find an active link to Amazon should you choose to order your textbook online.

Let's take a few moments to review course assignments and assessment information. Brief descriptions of all assignments are provided in the syllabus, and it is recommended that you read the assignment overview in detail on your own. In this review I will highlight:

- How to access course lectures and quizzes,
- The critical assignment for the course,
- Extra credit opportunities, and
- Course policies that you need to be aware of.

Lectures and lecture quizzes are contained in a learning object. Each week, you can access the lectures and quizzes by clicking on the name of the learning object and clicking "Click to Launch." This will open the learning object in a new window. Once the object is open, you can hover your mouse over the bottom edge of the object to reveal the object controls, such as a table of contents and closed captions.

The research paper is the critical assignment for this course. In order to receive a passing grade in the course, you must earn a minimum of 140 of a possible 200 points on the assignment. To assist you in passing the assignment, guided research paper activities have been incorporated into weeks one through five. As long as you meet the deadlines, I will personally give you feedback each week as you progress toward the completion of your research project.

For those of you on the lookout for extra credit opportunities, notice that two extra credit assignments are woven into the course. If you take a look at the "graded assignments" chart, you will see extra credit given for your course introduction and for completing the course evaluation at the end of the course.

Lastly, there are some important policies that you should be aware of:

- One—Use the APA style format for all writing assignments. While there are several websites with APA style examples, the definitive guide is the *APA Publication Manual*, 6th edition.

- Two—Your CBU e-mail address is the official form of e-mail communication. Should you need to e-mail me, please do so from your CBU e-mail so that I can reply to your CBU e-mail within twenty-four hours.

- Three—be sure to turn your work in on time to earn the highest marks for your completed assignments. While it is understood that many of you are working and managing families, you have chosen an accelerated course—meaning this fifteen-week course has been condensed into eight weeks. Nonetheless, you are still expected to complete nine hundred minutes of student engagement time each week. Late work will be accepted according to the policy stated in the syllabus. Please pay close attention to the point deduction.

- Lastly—It's probably a no-brainer that you are expected to complete your own work and to cite the ideas and quotes of others if you use them in written papers. If you are not familiar with the differences between summarizing, quoting, and paraphrasing, take a look at the information provided by the Online Writing Lab (OWL) of Purdue. A link to this webpage is provided in the week zero folder.

Should you have any questions regarding the course syllabus, feel free to contact me via e-mail or phone. I'll be happy to answer your questions or help you out any way that I can.

Appendix B

COURSE WELCOME AND ORIENTATION SCRIPT

This appendix presents a script used to welcome students to the course and orient them to a learning management system through a screencast video. It addresses recommended browser use, how to participate in discussions, how to upload assignments, and how to check grades.

COURSE WELCOME AND ORIENTATION SCRIPT FOR SCREENCAST

Welcome to SOC213, Introduction to Sociology. I'm Dr. Torria Bond, your instructor for this course. The purpose of this welcome is to help you navigate SOC213 in Blackboard and show you how to participate in Voice-Thread discussions and how to submit completed assignments in Blackboard. So, let's get started.

The first thing you should know is that Blackboard works best with Mozilla Firefox. So if you don't already have this particular browser on your computer, you can go to Mozilla.org or put Mozilla Firefox in the search field of your current browser and download the free internet browser. You don't have to replace Internet Explorer or Google Chrome, but you should experience fewer technical issues if you use Firefox with Blackboard. You should also make sure that you have the current version of Java on your computer. Java is required to access videos in Blackboard. Lastly, you want to make sure you are running the current version of Adobe Flash, as it is required to access interactive content in Blackboard.

Once you get to the course homepage, click on "Course Information" to access the "Getting Started" folder and the course syllabus, which we will review in a separate video. The learning activities link will take you to weekly modules. These weekly modules contain lectures, quizzes, and other instructional material. Upon entering a module, you will notice a table of contents, which contains active links you can use to browse the module's content. You can also use the directional arrows to the right of the content page to navigate through a module.

Let's discuss how to participate in VoiceThread discussions. The Voice-Thread player is embedded in the content page. In the lower left corner of the player you will see a "Sign In or Register" icon. Click this icon and register for your free account. Once your free account is established, you are ready to add a response to the VoiceThread. To do this, click "Comment". You will notice that there are multiple ways to comment. Clicking on the Record button will allow you to use your computer's microphone to leave a comment. After you leave a comment, you can save or cancel it. By clicking the Video icon, you can use your computer's webcam and microphone to leave a comment. Be sure to save the comment so that it will post to the VoiceThread. To comment on the responses of your peers' VoiceThread, click "Click to Launch" to access Blackboard's discussion features. Most discussions already have the required thread posted, and new threads may not be created. Enter a discussion thread and click "Reply". If you choose to, you may collapse the original post. In the subject area, add the name of the peer to whose VoiceThread response you are commenting, with a creative title that shares the essence of your comment. Type your comment in the text editor, then click "Submit". To reply to someone else's comment, click to open the comment, then click "Reply".

Now, let's discuss how to submit an assignment in Blackboard. Navigate to an assignment. After clicking the name of the assignment, you can access the assignment information and the assignment rubric, which details how the assignment will be evaluated. Below the "View Rubric" link is a text editor. Here you can type a comment that you might want me to see when I access your assignment. Below the text editor box is a "Browse My Computer" link. This link allows you to search your computer for the assignment file you want to upload. Once you have selected the assignment file from your computer, click "Submit". This will take you to a "Review Submission History" screen. If you have successfully submitted your assignment to Blackboard, you will see the date and time of submission, along with a link to the assignment file. To get off to a strong start, I recommend that you spend some time looking at the resources available in the "week zero" module. In week zero, you will find a blog to post an introduction of yourself. Here you will tell us your name, major, year in school, and you will upload a picture of your favorite meme.

You should also know about our online tutoring service, Smarthinking. Here you will have access to assistance whenever you need it in a variety of subjects. So don't hesitate to submit your papers to the writing center.

Lastly, let's click on the "Tools" link to access your grades through the "My Grades" link. Here you will find a list of graded assignments, points earned, points possible, assignment rubrics that explain how the assignment will be or was evaluated, and instructor comments.

If you have any other questions during our eight-week course, feel free to contact me. Please know that your success is my success. I'm here to help you with the technology, your assignments, and anything else you might need. So, welcome to SOC213—I'm looking forward to working with you.

REFERENCES

About Creative Commons. (n.d.). Creative Commons. Retrieved from http://creativecommons.org/

Akyol, Z., Garrison, D., and Ozden, M. (2009). Online and blended communities of inquiry: Exploring the developmental and perceptional differences. *International Review of Research in Open and Distance Learning, 10*(6), 65–83.

Allen, E. and Seaman, J. (2014). Grade change: Tracking online education in the United States. Retrieved from http://www.onlinelearningsurvey.com/reports/gradechange.pdf

American Library Association. (2014). Distance education and the TEACH act. Retrieved from http://www.ala.org/advocacy/copyright/teachact

Armstrong, D., Henson, K. & Savage, T. (2009). *Teaching today: An introduction to education.* Upper Saddle River, NJ: Merrill, an imprint of Pearson.

Bain, K. (2004). *What the best college teachers do.* Cambridge, MA: Harvard University Press.

Bandura, A. (1971). *Social learning theory.* New York, NY: General Learning Press.

Basketball Breakthrough. (2015). Basic basketball screens. Retrieved from https://www.breakthroughbasketball.com/articles/basic-basketball-screens.html

Berry, J. (2014). Easily amused: Big on the Web. Retrieved from http://johndberry.com/blog/2014/05/28/big-on-the-web/

Blackboard. (2013). Blackboard Exemplary Course Program Rubric. Retrieved from http://www.blackboard.com/resources/catalyst-awards /BbExemplaryCourseRubric_March2014.pdf

Bor, D. (2012). *The ravenous brain: How the new science of consciousness explains our insatiable search for meaning.* New York: Basic Books Publishing.

Brinton, D. & Holten , C. (1997). Into, through, and beyond: A framework to develop content-based material. Retrieved from http://dosfan.lib.uic .edu/usia/E-USIA/forum/vols/vol35/no4/p10.htm

Bruner, J., Goodnow, J. J., & Austin, G. A. (1967). *A study of thinking.* New York: Science Editions.

Center for Applied Special Technology (CAST). (2011). *Universal Design for Learning guidelines version 2.0.* Wakefield, MA: Author.

Conrad, R. & Donaldson, J. (2004). *Engaging the online learner: Activities and resources for creative instruction.* San Francisco, CA: Jossey-Bass.

Crews, K. (2010, April 2). The TEACH Act and some frequently asked questions. American Library Association. Retrieved from http://www.ala.org/advocacy/copyright/teachact/faq. doi:26c2dfac-12cc-4614-a90f-840fedfcdab5

Desilver, D. (2014). Overall book readership stable, but e-books becoming more popular. Retrieved from http://www.pewresearch.org/fact-tank/2014/01/21/ overall-book-readership-stable-but-e-books-becoming-more-popular/

Estes, T., Mintz, S. & Gunter, M. (2011). *Instruction: A models approach.* Boston, MA: Pearson.

Galleagher, S. (2012). *Concept development: A Hilda Taba teaching strategy.* Unionville, NY: Royal Fireworks Press.

Gottschall, H., & Garcia-Bayonas, M. (2008). Student attitudes toward group work among undergraduates in business administration, education, and mathematics. *Educational Research Quarterly, 1*(32), 3–28.

Greenfield, J. (2014). More Americans now reading ebooks, new pew data shows. Retrieved from http://www.digitalbookworld.com/2014/more-americans-now-reading-ebooks-new-pew-data-show/

Horton, W. (2012). *E-Learning by design*. San Francisco, CA: Pfeiffer, A Wiley Imprint.

Jenson, E. (2005). *Teaching with the brain in mind*. Alexandria, VA: Association for Supervision and Curriculum Development.

Lohr, L. (2008). *Creating graphics for learning and performance: Lessons in visual literacy*. Upper Saddle River, NJ: Pearson Education Inc.

Marzano, R. (2001). *Classroom instruction that works: Research-based strategies for increasing student achievement*. Alexandria, VA: Association for Supervision and Curriculum Development.

Orlando, J. (2010). Effective uses of video in the classroom. Retrieved from http://www.facultyfocus.com/articles/teaching-with-technology-articles/effective-uses-of-video-in-the-classroom/

Ornstein, A. & Hunkins, F. (2009). *Curriculum: Foundations, principles, and issues*. Boston, MA: Allyn and Bacon.

Pritchard, J. (2014, Feb. 11). TV comedian behind "Dumb Starbucks" in Los Angeles. Retrieved from http://bigstory.ap.org/article/starbucks-dumb-starbucks-store-not-ok

Schaefer, S. (2014, Feb. 11). Jokes on L.A.: Comedy Central behind Dumb Starbucks faux shop. Retrieved from http://www.latimes.com/local/lanow/la-me-ln-dumb-starbucks-comedy-central-20140210v-story.html

Suskie, L. (2009). *Assessing student learning: A common sense guide*. San Francisco: Jossey-Bass.

U.S. Copyright Office. (n.d.). Copyright Law of the United States of America and Related Laws Contained in Title 17 of the United States Code, Section 107, Limitations on Exclusive Rights: Fair Use. Retrieved from http://www.copyright.gov/title17/92chap1.html#107

USA.gov. (2015, Feb. 2). "What is a U.S. government work?" Retrieved from http://www.usa.gov/copyright.shtml

Vai, M., & Sosulski, K. (2011). *Essentials of online course design: A standards-based guide*. New York: Routledge.

Williams, R. (2008). *The non-designer's design book* (3rd ed.). Berkeley, CA: Peachpit Press.

INDEX

Page references followed by *fig* indicate an illustrated figure.

Case studies: Cirque du Soleil, 126–127*fig*; as interactive learning object, 125–126; intro sociology course design, 88–94*fig*

Center for Applied Special Technology, 5, 7

Charles Darwin University, 14

Checklists (discussion assignment), 69–70

Chunking, 102

Cirque du Soleil case study, 126–127*fig*

Classification: concept development model element of, 135–140; providing students with an interactive wall to post on, 137–140*fig*

Clip art, 8

Closed captions, 149–150

Collaboration: comparing interaction and, 64; definition of, 64; facilitating online discussions for, 64–65; Google presentation embedded in small group discussion space for, 74–75*fig*; teach students how to engage in online, 64, 67. *See also* Group assignments

Color/color scheme: Bloom's Taxonomy to facilitate color exploration simulation, 144, 145*fig*; color exploration simulation from website embedded in content page, 143, 144*fig*; legibility supported by selected, 141–144; sample rubric for designing set of content pages using, 152t; survey tool to elicit students' color preferences, 142*fig*

Concept attainment model: applied to the visual design module one, 133–135; basic design principles of the, 133–134; Blackboard test feature to implement the, 135, 136*fig*; description of, 132

Concept development model of instruction: applied to the visual design module one, 135–141; brainstorming strategy used with, 135, 136–137; description of, 132; instructor PowerPoint slides uploaded to VoiceThread on steps of, 137–140*fig*

Concepts: "chunking" new information on, 102; metaphor used to facilitate

recall of, 102–104; review student learning and prior knowledge about, 80*fig*–86

Conrad, R., 115, 130

Consistent design: beginning first content page with week's agenda for, 47*fig*; "Blended Course Design Tips" (Ombres) on using, 47–48; meaning-making facilitated through, 46–48; repeated content elements enhanced by visual cues, 48*fig*

Contacting instructors, 159*fig*–160

Content: chunking, 102; consistency of images and types of, 46–48*fig*; course design and importance of good, 131; create a link to external, 26; Creative Commons licenses for permission to display, 32*fig*, 35–36*fig*, 40, 60; deciding how much to include in lesson, 86; "hot mess" wth excessive amounts of, 1–4; icons used to visually distinguish different types of, 45–46*fig*; managing amount by combining video and forms, 84*fig*; problem of broken links to, 149–150; strategies to avoid overloading students with, 86–87; three ways to display video of, 57–59*fig*; visual design to make it accessible to diverse learners, 7, 149–150. *See also* Copyright infringement

Content folders: avoid including nice-to-know content in, 3, 90–91; example of "hot mess," 1–4, 21; high folder depth ratio taking away from learning, 4–5

Content items: building in an LMS, 8; integrate multimedia and similar, 20–21, 22*fig*; nice-to-know, 3, 90–91; PowerPoint file repurposed in web tool with embed code integrated into, 41*fig*; related instructional materials in one, 18*fig*; separate important but unrelated, 92–94*fig*; streamline related, 91–92*fig*, 134; Twitter information that includes integrating, 22*fig*. *See also* Links/linking

Content overload: merging reading objectives into quiz space to prevent,

92, 93*fig*; strategies to avoid, 86–87; streamline related content items to avoid, 91–92*fig*, 134

Content pages: Google Doc embedded on the, 137, 138*fig*; Google form embedded to collect student quiz responses on a, 74*fig*; the instructional page, 16–17, 18*fig*; interactive wall as focal point of the, 137, 139*fig*; keep the design L.I.T.E., 18–25*fig*; the landing page, 11–14*fig*, 148–149*fig*; link to external content from, 19–20*fig*, 22*fig*, 26; the navigation page, 14–16*fig*, 148–149*fig*, 162–163*fig*; rubric for cumulative activity of designing a set of, 152t; selecting color and color scheme for legibility of, 142–144*fig*, 145*fig*; the submission page, 17–18*fig*; three ways to display a video on a, 57–59*fig*; visual cues used to create consistency in the, 46–48*fig*; visual design module four on designing a set of three, 146–148; white space consideration for, 21–23*fig*, 99*fig*. *See also* Typography

Contrast design principle, 133, 134–135

Copyright: determining, 33–34*fig*; doctrine of fair use limitations on, 29, 30; legal definition of, 29; public domain versus, 29–30; TEACH Act governing educational and governmental use of works under, 31–32, 60. *See also* Creative Commons licenses

Copyright infringement: "Dumb Starbucks Coffee" parody as, 27–28; fair use exceptions to, 29, 30; four factors of, 30; "Happy Birthday" song, 27, 28; preventing problems with, 28–29. *See also* Content

Copyright Law of the United States of America, Circular 92, 34

Courier font, 23

Course design. *See* Online course design

Creative Commons licenses: description and purpose of, 32; Google search filtered by type of, 35–36*fig*; images available from free photo sharing and image sites with, 60; presentation web tools available under the, 40; representative icons depicting permissions granted through, 32*fig*. *See also* Copyright; Public domain

Cropping tool: description and using a, 38–39; to fit image in PowerPoint slide, 39*fig*

D

Davis, D., 155

DeLong, T. J., 126

Design principles: alignment, 133, 134–135; concept of development model to create content pages using four, 135–141; contrast (examples and non-examples), 133, 134–135; proximity, 133, 134–135; repetition, 133, 140–141; sample rubric for designing set of content pages using, 152t

Desilver, D., 98

Dewey, J., 130

Diagnostic assessment: interactive chart used as a, 111*fig*; visual design used for, 110–111

Digital badges, 42–43*fig*

Direct instruction lesson: background information on the, 76–77; deciding how much content to include, 86; L.I.T.E. visual Design Points used in, 77–86; Marshmallow Challenge exercise, 81–83; module entry point contains video message from instructor and lesson objectives, 78*fig*; objectives of the, 77–79*fig*; review previously learned material and identify prior knowledge, 80*fig*–86; strategies to avoid content overload, 86–87; a table used to manage alignment of text and video, 79*fig*; the word EMBED will be replaced with code in the HTML code view, 79*fig*

Direct instruction model: four steps to implement, 76; planning lesson using the, 76–87

Direct instruction steps: 1: provide context for the skill or principal being presented, 81–83; 2: present instructional information on how to perform skill, 83; 3: supervised practice and instructor feedback, 83–85*fig*; 4: provide learner with unsupervised activity to test knowledge, 85–86

Discussion forums: allow students to self-enroll in a small, 65–66; consider turning off permissions to create new threads, 68–69; give each forum a headline, 67–68*fig*; tool for student meme submissions to, 51*fig*; use a discussion rubric or checklist to evaluate participation, 69–70; video-based, 59–60*fig*. *See also* Online discussions

Discussion rubric or checklist, 69–70

Displaying multimedia: text editor view of the content page for, 100–101*fig*; use the table feature to format multimedia, 100, 101*fig*

Diverse learners: closed captions for, 149–150; style guides to enhance document navigation using assistive devices, 155, 156*fig*; visual design to make content accessible to, 7, 149–150

Doctrine of fair use, 29, 30

Donaldson, J., 115, 130

"Dumb Starbucks Coffee" parody, 27–28

Dunbar, S., 126

E

E-learning files: created in file manager and saved as zip file, 107*fig*; created using Camtasia and uploaded to instructor website, 110*fig*; extracting e-learning zip file, 108*fig*; html web page identified to create the URL from the, 109*fig*; web hosting service for instructor's, 106–107*fig*

Eastern Kentucky University, 76, 160

Ebook reading rates, 98

Education institutions: TEACH Act guidelines on use of copyrighted works by, 31–32, 60; Universal Design for Learning (UDL) framework use of, 5–6, 129

Embed/embedding: Blackboard text editor to embed codes into content page, 24–25*fig*; color exploration simulation from website embedded in content page, 143, 144*fig*; description of, 5; direct instruction lesson use of, 77–86; displaying multimedia by using, 100–101*fig*; embedding content in your course, 24; Google Doc on the content page, 137, 138*fig*; a Google form on a content page to collect student quiz responses, 74*fig*; a Google presentation in small group discussion space for collaboration, 74–75*fig*; links at the decision-making point of branching scenarios, 124; professor welcome video embedded into the landing page, 14*fig*. *See also* L.I.T.E. design skills

Embry-Riddle Aeronautical University, 51, 52

Emerson, M., 56, 57

Estes, T., 75, 76

Evans, K., 155

External content: link from content pages to, 19–20*fig*, 22*fig*, 26; LMS that allows you to create a link to, 26; Twitter information that includes links to, 22*fig*

F

Facebook groups: how to create a private, 161–162*fig*; providing assignment help through, 161

Fair use doctrine, 29, 30

Fangs Screen Reader Emulator, 155, 157*fig*

Fielder, N., 27

Flickr, 43

"Folder depth ratio," 4

Font styles/sizes: sample rubric for designing set of content pages using, 152t; selecting typefaces to promote readability, 144–146*fig*, 147*fig*; white space and, 21, 22, 23*fig*, 99

Formative assessment, 112–113*fig*

Forrest Gump (film), 88, 91

FTP upload features, 106

G

Gallagher, S., 132

Garcia-Bayonas, M., 66, 67, 70

Garrison, D., 7

Generalizations: concept development model element of synthesizing, 135–140; VoiceThread presentation used for synthesizing, 138–140*fig*

Geneva font, 23

Goodnow, J., 132

Google Docs: description of, 73; embedded on the content page, 137, 138*fig*; group brainstorming online on a shared, 131, 137, 138*fig*; group projects completed using, 73–74

Google searches: asking questions and getting answers using, 26; "create a room design," 126; filtered by the Creative Commons license "labeled for reuse," 36*fig*; filtering images by license type, 36*fig*; "free screen capture," 37; "grade book," 158; "learn html free," 100

Google Site: home page of a course built on, 116*fig*; learner engagement through, 115

Gottschall, H., 66, 67, 70

Government agencies: public domain of works produced by, 34*fig*; TEACH Act guidelines on use of copyrighted works by, 31–32, 60

Grade access tutorial, 158*fig*–159. *See also* Rubrics

"Grade Change: Tracking Online Education in the United States" (Allen and Seyman), 98

Graphic organizer, 145–146*fig*

Greenfield, J., 23, 98

Group assignments: discussion rubric or checklist to evaluate participation in, 69–70; Facebook or Twitter used to provide help with, 161–162*fig*; facilitate asynchronous discussion by team members, 66–67; online brainstorming on, 131, 137; providing students with the opportunity to work on, 66; teach students how to

collaborate online in, 67. *See also* Assignments; Collaboration

Group projects: first of four parts of a major eight-week course, 72*fig*; Google Docs used for, 73–74; Google form embedded on a content page to collect student quiz responses, 74*fig*; group space prepared in advance for the four conversations needed to complete the, 73*fig*; online planning of, 70–71; scaffold multifaceted projects, 71–74

Gunter, M., 75, 76

H

"Happy Birthday" song, 27, 28

Heading styles, 23, 155, 156*fig*

Helvetica font, 23

Henson, K., 63

Holten, C., 141

Horton, W., 64

"Hot mess" content folder: example of, 1–2*fig*; four reasons why it is a, 2–3; high folder depth ratio contributing to, 4–5

HTML icon (Blackboard), 25*fig*

HTML learning resources, 100

HTML tutorial (W3Schools.Com), 100

Hunkins, F., 63, 130

I

Icons: Blackboard text editor HTML, 24–25*fig*; creating visual cues through, 45–46*fig*; Creative Commons licenses and representative, 32*fig*; Microsoft Office Online Pictures, 8, 9*fig*

Idaho Digital Learning Academy, 33

Image applications: to create a welcoming course environment, 44*fig*–45; displaying video, 57–59*fig*; to establish positive learning community, 48–50*fig*; incorporating video in online instruction, 53–54*fig*, 55; to motivate and encourage students, 42–43*fig*; screencasting, 55–57; using consistent types of content, 46–48*fig*; video-based discussion forum,

Integrate/integrating multimedia: adding multimedia to instructional scenario, 120, 122–123; description of, 5; direct instruction lesson use of, 77–79*fig*; integrating SCORM files into LMS, 104–107*fig*, 108*fig*, 109*fig*, 110*fig*; interactive learning objectives, 124–127*fig*; legibility issue of, 98*fig*–100, 141–144*fig*, 145*fig*; as L.I.T.E. skill, 5, 18; managing content items using, 20–21, 22*fig*; readability issue of, 21–23*fig*, 98*fig*–100; strategies for displaying multimedia, 100–101*fig*; Twitter information that includes, 22*fig*; using multimedia for assessment, 107–110; visual design for diagnostic assessment, 110–111. *See also* L.I.T.E. design skills

Intellectual property: copyright infringement of, 27–29, 30; Creative Commons licenses to use works of, 32*fig*, 33*fig*; doctrine of fair use applied to, 29, 30; TEACH Act guidelines on educational and governmental use of, 31–32, 60

Interaction: comparing collaboration and, 64; definition of, 64; facilitating online discussions for, 64–65

Interactive learning objectives: case studies used as, 125–126; description and learning value of, 124–125; draft of one scene from the, 126–127*fig*

"Into, through, and beyond" model, 141–144*fig*

Intro sociology course design case study: eliminate nice-to-know content items, 90–91; learn to minimize the use of new technologies, 90; merging reading objectives into quiz space to prevent content overload, 92, 93*fig*; separate important but unrelated content items, 92–94; streamline related content items, 91–92*fig*; week one overview (L.I.T.E. revision) with reduced content, 94*fig*; week one overview (original M.E.S.S.) with excessive content, 88–89*fig*

Instructional models. *See* Inquiry models of instruction

Iowa State University, 100

J

Jenson, E., 102
Jing, 37–38*fig*, 81

K

Kappers, W., 47
KWL assessment strategy, 111

L

Lake Sumter State College (Florida), 155

Landing pages: characteristics of a well-designed, 12–14; creating presence on, 148–149*fig*; description of the, 11–12; designing a, 11–14; example of an online course, 13*fig*; professor welcome video embedded into the, 14*fig*

Laubengayer, K., 33

Learner engagement: facilitating asynchronous, 66–67; instructor role in facilitating online discussion and, 64–65; multimedia strategies for, 115–116*fig*; rubric or checklist for discussion participation, 69–70

Learner support: facilitating contact with the instructor, 159*fig*–160; facilitating student use of course features, 162–164*fig*; facilitating student use of the syllabus as, 154–157; importance of providing, 153–154; providing help with assignments, 161–162*fig*; providing help with the technology, 160–161*fig*; tracking student progress throughout the course, 157–159

Learners: allow them to self-enroll in a small discussion group, 65–66; discussion rubric or checklist to evaluate participation by, 69–70; graphic organizer to facilitate independent exploration, 145–146*fig*; images used to motivate and encourage, 42–43*fig*; instructor learning support of, 7; positive learning community through creative introductions, 49–50*fig*; reviewing previously learned material and prior knowledge of, 80–86; screen shot tutorial on how to access grades and instructor feedback, 158*fig*–159; teaching them how to collaborate online, 67. *See also* Learning outcomes

Learning communities: images used to establish positive, 48–50*fig*; instructor role in the, 7; sharing perspectives with other learners in the course, 7

Learning management systems (LMSs): building a content item in, 8; challenge of storing multimedia files on, 104; features that you need to have in an, 25–26; integrating SCORM files into, 104–107*fig*, 108*fig*, 109*fig*, 110*fig*; PowerPoint file repurposed in web tool with embed code integrated into, 41; Secure Socket Layer (SSL) certificate for secure communication with, 106. *See also* Blackboard; Online course design

Learning outcomes: assessment of, 107–115; creating a course orientation video that goes over the, 56–57; high folder depth ratio takes away from, 4–5; how a "hot mess" design takes away from, 1–4; image displays to showcase lesson objectives and, 50–53; keeping course design light to focus on, 4–6; reviewing prior knowledge and previously learned materials, 80–86; using multimedia for instruction and, 102–107*fig*. *See also* Learners

Legibility: typography and design for, 98*fig*–100; visual design module two on color schemes that support, 141–144*fig*, 145*fig*

Lesson objectives: direct instruction lesson, 77–79*fig*; displayed on an instructional content page, 16*fig*; displayed on entrance to the learning module, 133*fig*; images display to showcase learning outcomes and,

50–53; visual design module one, 132; visual design module two, 141; visual design module three, 144; visual design module four, 146

Lesson planning: challenges associated with, 63; direct instruction lesson using direct instruction model, 76–87. *See also* Online instruction

Links/linking: content page link to external content, 19–20*fig*, 22*fig*, 26; create a link to external content, 26; at the decision-making point of branching scenarios, 124; description of, 5; direct instruction lesson use of, 78*fig*–79*fig*; instructional content page, 14, 16*fig*; as L.I.T.E. skill, 5, 18; navigation content page, 14, 15*fig*; problem of broken, 149–150; syllabus, 14. *See also* Content items; L.I.T.E. design skills

L.I.T.E. design skills: introduction to embed, 5; introduction to integrate multimedia, 5; introduction to links, 5; introduction to typography, 5. *See also specific skill*

L.I.T.E. Visual Design Points: avoiding a M.E.S.S. by using, 18–19, 21, 129; creating content pages with, 18–25*fig*; direct instruction lesson use of, 77–79*fig*; intro sociology course: week one overview improvement through, 94*fig*; Marshmallow Challenge exercise use of, 81–83; repurposing M.E.S.S. by using, 87; supporting visual design with, 6–7; UDL framework complemented with, 5–6, 129. *See also* Online courses; Visual design

Lloyd, C., 59

Lohr, L., 133

M

Marshmallow Challenge exercise: blog space for students to report on the, 82*fig*–83; description of and L.I.T.E. Visual Design Points used for, 81–83; PowerPoint presentation of, 81, 82*fig*

Marzano, R., 102

Massive open online course (MOOC): creating small discussion groups out of, 65–66; large number of students enrolled in, 65

Meaning-making: consistent types of content to facilitate, 47*fig*–48*fig*; the human brain process of, 46–47

Memes: discussion board tool for student submissions of, 51*fig*; student-created introduction using, 50*fig*

M.E.S.S. design: example of a "hot mess" or, 1–4, 21; example of poorly done information on Twitter, 2*fig*, 21; of the intro sociology course case study, 88–90; L.I.T.E. skills to help avoid a, 18–19, 21, 129; L.I.T.E. to repurpose, 87

Metaphor: applied to facilitate recall, 103–104; description and function of a, 102–103; Venn diagram used to apply to recall, 104, 105*fig*

Microsoft Office Suite: Online Picture icon in, 9*fig*; style guides to enhance document navigation using assistive devices, 155, 156*fig*; visual images available through, 8–9*fig*

Microsoft PowerPoint: building a content item in, 8; concept attainment model and building examples/non-examples in, 134–135; converting a PowerPoint file into a video file, 122–123; creating a soft-edge effect on a portrait in, 12; creating branching scenarios responsive to user input in, 123–124*fig*, 125*fig*; cropping images to fit in slide, 38–39*fig*; instructor file repurposed in web tool with embed code into content item, 41*fig*; Marshmallow Challenge exercise presentation on, 81–82*fig*; as presentation web tool, 40–41*fig*; removing image backgrounds for transparent background in, 8, 9*fig*; slides uploaded to Voice Thread on the concept development model, 137–138, 139*fig*; storyboard learning scenario in, 120, 121*fig*, 122*fig*;

visual images available through, 8–9; WordArt to create typography in, 80*fig*–81, 84

Mintz, S., 75, 76

MLA (Modern Language Association), 23

Module splash page, 51–52*fig*

Morris, E., 55

Mozilla's OpenBadges site, 42

MP4 video format, 55, 56, 122–123

Multimedia: adding to the scenario, 120, 122–123; challenge of storing files on LMS, 104; converting a PowerPoint file into a video file, 122–123; interactive learning objectives, 124–127*fig*; learner management using, 115–116*fig*; legibility issue of, 98*fig*–100, 141–144*fig*, 145*fig*; readability issue of, 21–23*fig*, 98*fig*–100; strategies for displaying, 100–101*fig*; use for instruction, 102–107*fig*; using for assessment, 107–110; visual design for diagnostic assessment, 110–111

N

Nadolyny, L., 100

Navigation pages: creating presence on, 148–149*fig*; description and function of, 14–15; links in a table of content, 14, 16*fig*; links on a sidebar on a, 14, 15*fig*; screenshot tutorial explaining course navigation, 162–163*fig*

Neal, J. G., 51, 52

Newcastle University (UK), 162

Nice-to-know content items: avoid including, 3; intro sociology course design case study on eliminating, 90–91

Northern Illinois University, 159–160

O

Obama, Barack, 34

Objectives: displayed on an instructional content page, 16*fig*; images display to showcase learning outcomes and lesson, 50–53; where to locate course, 17

Old English font, 143

Ombres, S., 47

Online and Professional Studies Division (CBU), 40, 42, 43, 55, 56, 59, 60, 113, 119, 126, 155

Online course design: case study on intro sociology course on instructional, 88–94*fig*; content pages, 11–25*fig*; displaying images, 37–46*fig*; example of "hot mess" content folder, 1–4; four basic design principles and examples/non-examples, 133–141; good content as essential to, 131; keeping it light to facilitate learning outcomes, 4–6; learning to create visual images in, 8–11; L.I.T.E. foundational skills for, 5–7; preventing copyright infringement in your, 28–29; removing distractions from the online environment, 7. *See also* Learning management systems (LMSs); L.I.T.E. Visual Design Points

Online courses: facilitating student use of features of the, 162–164*fig*; the future and potential of, 164–165; home page of course build on Google site, 116*fig*; increasing rate of students taking, 98; intro sociology course case study, 88–94*fig*; tracking student progress throughout the, 157–159

Online discussions: consider turning off permissions to create new threads, 68–69; facilitating asynchronous, 66–67; instructor facilitation of, 64–65; strategy for preparing learners for a topic on asynchronous, 110–111*fig*; teach students how to collaborate through, 64, 67; use a discussion rubric or checklist to evaluate participation, 69–70. *See also* Discussion forums

Online environment: examples of four ways to create visuals in, 10*fig*; good design used to remove distractions from, 7; images used as digital badges to students in an, 42–43*fig*; images used to create a welcoming, 44*fig*–45; steps for creating images in an, 9, 11

Online instruction: case study on instructional design of intro sociology course, 88–94*fig*; direct instruction lesson using direct instruction for, 76–87; examining the different options for improving, 75–76; incorporating video into, 53–54*fig*, 55; interactive learning objects used for, 124–127*fig*; learning scenarios used as part of, 116–124*fig*, 125*fig*; using multimedia for, 102–107*fig*. *See also* Inquiry models of instruction; Instructors; Lesson planning

Online Learning Consortium's "Successful Online Outcomes: Improved Discussions," 65

Orlando, J., 86

Ornstein, A., 63, 130

O'Rourke, M., 119

Ozden, M., 7

P

Padlet, 111

Papanek, V., 63

Pappas, C., 97

Perkins, J., 76, 160

Pew Research Foundation ebook reading report (2011 to 2014), 98

Photographs: creating a soft-edge effect in PowerPoint, 12; landing page instructor, 11–12. *See also* Images

Piaget, J., 130

Plagiarism, 40

Positive learning community: importance of establishing a, 48–50; student-created meme submitted for course introductions, 49–50*fig*

PowerPoint. *See* Microsoft PowerPoint

Presence: contacting instructors and issue of, 159*fig*–160; using same landing page and navigational page to establish, 148–149*fig*; visual design used to create a sense of, 7, 148. *See also* Instructors